SECOND EDITION 6

Super Practice Book

SUPER PRACTICE

Garan Holcombe

CAMBRIDGE
UNIVERSITY PRESS

Map of the book

Present perfect with *already* / *yet* revision

Language focus

Use present perfect with **already** to talk about actions which have happened before now. **Already** means 'before now' or 'before this time'.

This is the form of the sentence: **has** / **have** + **already** + **past participle**.

Dad ***has already painted*** *that fence!*

Already is also used to express surprise that something has happened sooner than expected.

Sophia is only 12 but she has ***already*** *lived in Istanbul, Madrid, Beijing and Paris.*

Oscar is only 11 but he has ***already*** *learned to play the violin, piano, guitar and trumpet.*

Use **present perfect** with **yet** to talk about actions which haven't happened up to now. **Yet** means 'up to now' or 'up to this moment in time'. We often use it to talk about something we haven't done but expect to do.

This is the form of the sentence: **hasn't** / **haven't** + **past participle** + **yet**.

Have you played *on the new tennis courts yet?* *Yes, I have, but I* ***haven't played*** *on the new basketball courts* ***yet****.*

1 **Write the past participles.**

1 become ___became___
2 begin ______
3 catch ______
4 get ______
5 send ______
6 meet ______
7 understand ______
8 win ______

2 Complete the questions with the verbs from the box in the correct form.

see ~~have~~ go fix finish call

1 Have you ___had___ lunch yet?
2 Have you ______ your homework yet?
3 Have your friends ______ the new Star Wars film yet?
4 Have you ______ your grandmother yet?
5 Has Dad ______ my bike yet?
6 Have you ______ to the supermarket yet?

3 Correct the sentences.

1 Have you tidies your room yet?
Have you tidied your room yet?
2 Marco has already score ten goals for the team this year.
______
3 I yet haven't had my lunch.
______
4 We hasn't been to the new museum yet.
______
5 I have had something already to eat.
______
6 Paula have already finished her English project.
______

4 Make sentences in the present perfect using *yet, already* and the verbs from the box.

learn be try visit read ~~do~~ see play

1 I haven't done my homework yet.
2 ______
3 ______
4 ______
5 ______
6 ______
7 ______
8 ______

who / which / where revision

Language focus

Who / **which** / **where** are relative pronouns. Use these words to give more information about a person (**who**), thing (**which**) or place (**where**).

*Frank is the boy **who** won the school's painting competition.*

*Football is the sport **which** I enjoy the most.*

*Izmir is the city **where** my friend Ecem was born.*

1 **Complete the sentences with *who, which* or *where*.**

1 The city ___which___ I like the best is Madrid.
2 My sister is the person __________ has taught me the most.
3 The place __________ I am happiest is my bedroom.
4 The thing __________ I like the most is my snowboard.
5 The sport __________ I play all the time is basketball.
6 The people __________ I love the most are my parents and my brother.
7 The films __________ I enjoy the most are full of action and adventure.
8 The hospital __________ I was born is very near my house.

2 Put the words in the correct order to complete the sentences.

1 the / never / watch / sport / I / which / .
Tennis is **the sport which I never watch.**

2 most / go / I / where / the / often / place / .
The school's music room is ______

3 me / most / important / to / the / is / which / .
My bracelet is the thing ______

4 no one / except / the / where / can / go / me / room / .
My bedroom is ______

5 who / English / the / student / best / speaks / the / .
Alberto is ______

3 Circle the correct relative pronoun.

1 The football pitch ______ we play all our matches is on the other side of town.
a which (b) where

2 The girl ______ lives opposite us is from Barcelona.
a who b where

3 The wood next to our house is the place ______ I take the dog for a walk.
a which b where

4 Istanbul is the city ______ my uncle and aunt live.
a who b where

5 The strawberry cake ______ my brother made for me was delicious.
a which b who

6 The boy ______ joined our class last week is from Brazil.
a who b which

4 Correct the sentences.

1 Yang is the boy where comes from Shanghai.
Yang is the boy who comes from Shanghai.

2 The park which we play is near my school.
______

3 The motorbike who my sister bought is a Yamaha.
______

4 History is the subject where I enjoy the most.
______

5 Marta and Alba are the people where I like to be with all the time.
______

Reading: a school newsletter

1 **Read the newsletter and write *t* (true) or *f* (false). Correct the false sentences.**

The Alan Turing High School Newsletter

Big changes for next year!

Football, bikes and running

Many things will be different at school next year. Students who love playing football will really enjoy our amazing new pitch, while those of you who want to join the running club will enjoy the new track we have already put in. We've also got lots of extra bike racks where the old Science room used to be and we would really like to see more of you cycling to school next term.

The railings

We haven't repaired the railings at the entrance which were damaged in the storms last winter yet, but you should find that everything looks bright and clean ready for the start of the new term.

Saved by the new bell!

Our old school bell was not very popular. Almost every day someone said, 'It's too noisy.' For that reason, we have a new bell which we will test on the first morning to make sure everyone knows the new sound.

Anyone for tennis?

We are delighted to welcome Miss Kulin to the school. She will be our first tennis coach. Miss Kulin is an ex-professional tennis player who played for five years on the tour. She will run the after-school tennis club three nights a week.

1 The school hasn't got a new football pitch.
[f] *The school has got a new football pitch.*

2 There aren't any new bike racks at the school.
[ ] ______

3 The school wants more students to use their bikes.
[ ] ______

4 The railings haven't been fixed yet.
[ ] ______

5 Everyone liked the old school bell.
[ ] ______

6 Miss Kulin has never played tennis professionally.
[ ] ______

Writing

1 **Complete the sentences with the words from the box.**

teacher trip ~~changes~~ online week

1 We would like to tell you about some big changes at the school.
2 We look forward to welcoming our new ______________.
3 We've had a wonderful ______________ at the school.
4 We hope all our students enjoy the skiing ______________ at the weekend.
5 Students who want to join the running club can sign up ______________.

Help with Writing

School newsletters are usually sent out daily or weekly. They tell parents and students about competitions and prizes, new teachers, new facilities and future trips. Newsletters are written in a formal but friendly style.

2 **You are the principal of Valley High School. There are some changes you would like to tell parents about in the latest newsletter. Use the Reading page and the sentences in Activity 1 to help you write your newsletter. Include information about the following:**

- teachers (name, the subject each person teaches)
- facilities (e.g. bike racks, basketball hoops, running track)
- after-school clubs (e.g. tennis club, running club, football club).

Listening: a new school

1 01 **Listen to George talk to his mum. Write *t* (true) or *f* (false).**

1 George has already packed his schoolbag. [t]
2 George's class has got only one teacher. [ ]
3 Mr Martin teaches George's class one day a week. [ ]
4 There's a box where students put their homework on Mondays. [ ]
5 George and his mum have already met Katy. [ ]
6 George hasn't made his bed yet. [ ]

2 02 **What has George's new school got? Listen and tick ✓ or cross ✗.**

Welcome to your new school!

Come and enjoy these facilities:

- a running track ✓
- a football pitch ☐
- tennis courts ☐
- a playground with basket hoops ☐
- a gym ☐
- a library ☐
- bike racks ☐

Speaking

1 Work with a friend. Look at the school facilities. Play the guessing game.

Is this a place where you play computer games?

No, it isn't.

Is this a place where you play an instrument?

Yes, it is! It's a music room!

gym

computer room

tennis court

running track

library

music room

2 Think of your perfect school. Write answers. Then practise.

1 Where is your school? ________________

2 What do you learn there? ________________

3 What facilities has your school got? ________________

4 What is your favourite place at the school? Why? ________________

____

3 Work with a friend. Talk about your perfect school.

My perfect school is in the countryside. It's next to a lake where you can swim! You can learn languages at my school.

Can you do sport there too?

Yes! It's got a football pitch, a tennis court and a big library, but my favourite place is the farm. I love animals and I can look after them there.

1 Present perfect with *for* and *since*

Inma and Alvaro have been friends **since** they were three years old.

Language focus

Use **present perfect** with **for** and **since** to talk about actions or states which began in the past and continue until the present.

Use **for** to talk about a period of time, e.g. one day, two weeks, three months, four years.

Henry has lived in San Francisco ***for*** *ten years.*

Use **since** to talk about a point in time, e.g. last year, 2014, my birthday, this morning.

Katie has played the saxophone ***since*** *the beginning of the year.*

1 **Write *for* or *since*.**

1 six weeks ___for___
2 last weekend ______
3 this morning ______
4 two days ______
5 2015 ______
6 five minutes ______
7 December ______
8 last Friday ______
9 half an hour ______
10 eight months ______

2 Circle the correct word.

1 Our school football team has won the league *for* / *since* the last three years.
2 My mother has been a clothes designer *for* / *since* 20 years.
3 My friend Sam has played the piano *for* / *since* he was five years old.
4 We've lived in this house *for* / *since* 2009.
5 My sister lived in Santiago de Chile *for* / *since* six months.
6 My brother has been interested in dinosaurs *for* / *since* he was a little boy.

3 Complete the text messages with *for* or *since*.

Hi, Alex. We've been here (1) **for** a week. It's great! I don't want to leave.

I want to be you! I've been in bed with a really bad cold (2) ___________ Monday.

Oh no! I'm sorry to hear that. Get better soon. I probably shouldn't tell you – I've been on the beach (3) ___________ we got here!

No, you shouldn't! Text me when you get home. You can come round to see my new phone. I've had it (4) ___________ a week. It's got a great screen!

Lucky you! I'd love a new phone. I've had mine (5) ___________ ages!

Yes, I know. You've had yours (6) ___________ we were in our old school. I'm going to say goodbye now. I need to go back to sleep. Enjoy the rest of your holiday!

4 Complete the sentences with *for* or *since* and a time expression.

1 I've studied English ______________________________.
2 I've lived in my house ______________________________.
3 I've known my best friend ______________________________.
4 I've been at my school ______________________________.
5 I haven't tidied my room ______________________________.
6 I haven't gone on holiday ______________________________.

How long have you ... ?

Language focus

Use **How long have you ... ?** to ask about the length of time someone has been doing or had something.

How long have you *had your motorbike?*

In response to the question, you can use either **for** or **since**.

I've had my bike ***for*** *five years* or *I've had my bike* ***since*** *2016.*

1 **Correct the questions.**

1 How long have you speaking Chinese?

How long have you spoken Chinese?

2 How longs have you lived in your flat?

3 Who long has your mother worked at the university?

4 How long has your brother be a police officer?

5 How long having you had a dog?

6 How long has you owned this piano?

2 Complete the questions with the verbs from the box in the correct form.

study live have know ~~play~~ be (x2) work

1 How long has your sister ___played___ the guitar?
2 How long has your mother ______ a journalist?
3 How long have you ______ in your house?
4 How long have you ______ your tablet?
5 How long has your father ______ as a doctor?
6 How long has your brother ______ Anthony?
7 How long have you ______ Arabic?
8 How long have your grandparents ______ dance champions?

3 Match the questions from Activity 2 with answers a–h.

a For about two years. They dance every day! ___
b Since September. It's not easy to learn, but I'm enjoying it. ___
c For two months. She got a Fender for her birthday. ___1___
d For a few days. I love it! It's much better than my laptop. ___
e Since she left university. ___
f For a long time. They started playing football together when they were about five years old. ___
g For almost 20 years. He loves his job. ___
h Since 2014. We love living here. ___

4 Write questions with *How long have / has* and *you / he / she … ?*

1 How long have you known John?
I've known John since we were four years old.

2 ______
She's lived in Rome for two years.

3 ______
He's been a teacher for four years.

4 ______
I've lived in my house since I was three.

5 ______
He's played basketball since 2013.

6 ______
I've been here for 20 minutes.

Reading: an email to ask for information

1 **Read the email and circle the correct words to complete the sentences.**

To: fleurjack@treasureisland.com

Subject: Request for information

Dear Fleur Jack,

I am writing to ask you for some information about your Treasure Island theme park. I have written several emails before this one, but I haven't had a reply.

My friends and I have all been interested in pirates since we were young, and we are very excited about exploring Treasure Island, especially about seeing the hammocks, treasure chests, palm trees and gold coins the photographs on your website show.

We have taken a good look at your website, but there are some questions that I couldn't find the answers to online. First of all, is there a discount for groups? There will be five of us on the day: two adults and three children. Secondly, are the rides safe for children of all ages? Finally, I couldn't see how close the train station was to the park. Is it a short walk or would we have to take a taxi?

By the way, how long has Treasure Island been open? A friend of mine says that the park has been open for two years. Is that true?

I look forward to hearing from you.

Best wishes,

Steven Robertson

1 Steven and his friends have been interested in pirates for *a long time* / *a few weeks.*
2 Steven *has written a few emails* / *has written only one email* to staff at the Treasure Island theme park.
3 Steven *has had* / *hasn't had* an email from Fleur.
4 Steven says that a group of *three* / *five* will go to the theme park.
5 Steven *doesn't ask* / *asks* about getting to the theme park.
6 Steven *doesn't know* / *knows* when the theme park opened.

1 **Look at the email on the Reading page again. Complete the table with phrases used in formal emails.**

A way of beginning an email	Dear
Explaining the reason for writing the email	
Changing the subject in an email	
Introducing points or questions	
A sentence to say you'd like a reply	
A phrase to end an email	

Help with Writing

When writing a formal email, make sure you include a subject line. This helps to make everything as clear as possible. Make the subject line short but easy to understand.

2 **Write an email to Fleur Jack at the Treasure Island theme park. Use the phrases from Activity 1. Include the following:**

- Say how long you have enjoyed pirate stories.
- Ask how much the tickets are.
- Ask how long the park has been open.
- Ask if there is a café.

Listening: pirates

1 03 **Listen to the story. Complete the sentences.**

1 One morning, Master Bob was having a rest in his hammock.

2 Samuel used his ____________ to scratch his head.

3 The pirates loved to find ____________ ____________ on different beaches.

4 They also liked relaxing under ____________ ____________.

5 Master Bob wanted some new ____________ ____________ to be happy.

6 Mary Ann of the North climbed onto the ship. She was wearing a blue ____________.

2 04 **Listen to the conversation. Answer the questions.**

1 What is Freddie's show called?
It's called 'Pirates'.

2 How long has he been practising for the show?
____

3 How old was Freddie when he started drama club?
____

4 How many plays has he been in since he started acting?
____

5 Does Helen go to the theatre often?
____

6 Which day can Helen go to see Freddie's show?
____

1 **Work with a friend. Choose one pirate each. Make questions about your pirates using the words in the box. Then ask and answer.**

1 what / called?
2 how old?
3 what / look like?
4 what / doing?
5 how long / pirate?

What's your pirate called?

He's called Bluebeard.

Bluebeard
42 years old
pirate for 20 years

Elizabeth L.
35 years old
pirate for 15 years

Help with Speaking

When you have to ask questions, think about them first. You can write them on a piece of paper if you need to. Look at your friend as you ask each of your questions and give them time to answer.

2 **Draw a picture of a pirate. Complete the sentences and practise.**

This is my pirate. He's / She's called ________________ and he's / she's ______ years old. He's / She's wearing ____________________________, and he's / she's got ____________________________. In the picture, my pirate is ______________________. ________________ has been a pirate for ______ years.

3 **Talk about your pirate.**

This is my pirate. She's called Flora Morgan and she's 30 years old. She's wearing a red hat and she's got a pair of binoculars. In the picture, my pirate is standing on her ship. Flora Morgan has been a pirate for ten years.

2 need to

Language focus

Use **need to** to talk about something that is necessary or an obligation.

*I **need to** study hard tonight. I've got a Science test tomorrow morning.*

Use the negative form, **don't need to**, to say that something is not necessary or is not an obligation.

*You **don't need to** bring any food. We've already prepared an enormous picnic.*

1 **Complete the sentences with the verbs from the box.**

read ~~work~~ exercise go practise get

1 You need to ___work___ hard to pass your exams.
2 You need to ________ every day to play a musical instrument well.
3 You need to ________ to university to be a doctor.
4 You need to ________ a good night's sleep to have lots of energy the next day.
5 You need to ________ regularly to be strong and healthy.
6 You need to ________ a lot to increase your vocabulary.

2 Match 1–6 with a–f.

1 You don't need to tidy up.
2 You don't need to take a tent on the trip.
3 You don't need to catch the bus.
4 You don't need to tell Andy or Julia about the concert.
5 You don't need to bring anything.
6 You don't need to get up early.

a We've got everything we need for the picnic. ____
b Mum will take you home. ____
c I texted them earlier. ____
d I'll do it later. __1__
e We're not going until after lunch. ____
f They give you one at the campsite. ____

3 Complete the sentences with *need to* or *don't need to.*

1 You __need to__ bring a coat, hat and scarf. It's going to be cold!
2 You ________ buy any milk. I got some this morning.
3 We ________ go or we'll miss the bus!
4 You ________ check the train times. I've already got them on my phone.
5 If you're going out, you ________ put sun cream on. It's hot today.
6 We ________ buy tickets online. We can get them at the cinema.
7 I ________ call Grandad and wish him a happy birthday.
8 Come on! We ________ score or we'll lose the match.

4 Write about what you need to do and don't need to do this week.

1 ____
____
2 ____
____
3 ____
____
4 ____
____
5 ____
____

will / won't

Language focus

Use **will** / **won't** to make predictions. (A prediction refers to something we think will happen in the future.) After **will** / **won't**, use the **infinitive without to**.

We ***will travel*** *to other planets, but we* ***won't live*** *on them.*

We often use the contracted form of **will** after pronouns:

I will	– ***I'll***	*it will*	– ***it'll***
you will	– ***you'll***	*we will*	– ***we'll***
he will	– ***he'll***	*you will*	– ***you'll***
she will	– ***she'll***	*they will*	– ***they'll***

Yes/No question form	Short answers
Will we travel by jet pack one day?	*Yes, we* ***will****. / No, we* ***won't****.*
Will there be food for all the world's people?	*Yes, there* ***will****. / No, there* ***won't****.*

'Wh' question form

What will the world be like in 3000? — *I think it* ***will be*** *like a science-fiction film.*

1 **Complete the sentences with the verbs from the box.**

use ~~travel~~ work stop read eat

1 How will we **travel** in 2050?
2 Will we ______ using the Internet one day?
3 We will ______ healthier food.
4 We won't ______ books any more.
5 We won't ______ in offices.
6 We will ______ robots in our homes.

2 **Rewrite the predictions using contractions.**

1 You will go to Cambridge University.
You'll go to Cambridge University.
2 We will win the league next year.
______
3 They will make lots of money.
______
4 He will be a famous actor.
______
5 She will get top marks in her exams.
______
6 I will climb Mount Everest.
______

3 **Answer the questions with your own ideas, using short answers.**

1 Will we travel to Mars? ______
2 Will we replace the Internet with a new technology? ______
3 Will we stop eating meat? ______
4 Will there be more extreme weather like storms and floods? ______
5 Will people stop watching football? ______
6 Will we be less interested in famous people? ______

4 **Make your own predictions. Complete the sentences with *will* or *won't*.**

1 There ______ be computers in tables, walls, trees and roads.
2 Most people ______ live until they are 150 years old.
3 We ______ live on the moon.
4 There ______ be driverless cars.
5 China ______ win the football World Cup.
6 People ______ be happier.

Reading: an advertisement

1 **Read the advertisement and complete the table.**

Drive the future

Do you need a new car? Yes, you do! We all need something new once in a while. And the newest thing on the planet is our beautiful flying car – yes, that's right, the world's first flying car.

You won't believe how good it feels to fly a car. We know – we've tried it. Buy a **Zipwing+** today and this will be your future:

- You will avoid traffic jams.
- You will look down on the busy roads and smile.
- You will see our towns and cities from above.
- You will have the sky to yourself.

The **Zipwing+** has a solar-panel covering and comes with two top-of-the-range parachutes. Floating 10 metres above the ground, the **Zipwing+** can reach a maximum speed of 40 kilometres per hour and it will only get faster as we work hard on the latest designs and engines.

What are you waiting for? Come and test-fly one today. If you like what you see, the **Zipwing+** can be yours for a very special price – all that technology for only £500,000, down from the usual price of £750,000!

To book a test flight visit www.zipwing-plus.com

Name of the car	The Zipwing+
What is different about the car	
How fast the car can go	
How much the car is	

Help with Writing

Slogans are short phrases which usually go at the top of an advert. The job of a slogan is to sell a product to someone by making an idea stay in their mind. Slogans need to be short as well as interesting, funny or unusual.

1 Match 1–5 with a–e to make slogans for car adverts.

1 This is the	a to see this car	____
2 Will you	b drive the future?	____
3 You need to	c car of the future.	1
4 The future of the car is in	d the air.	____
5 We need you	e see this car to believe it.	____

2 Write an advertisement for a car of the future. Include a slogan as well as the following information:

- the name of the car
- what the car can do that is different
- how the buyer's life will be better with the car
- how much the car costs
- where you can buy the car.

Listening: travel

1 05 **Listen to Professor Lucy Mayweather. What does she think? Circle the correct words.**

1 We will travel *more* / *less* in the future.
2 Cars and *bikes* / *planes* are bad for the planet.
3 People *will* / *won't* need cars and planes to travel.
4 We won't make *long* / *short* trips in the future.
5 People will get around by cable car, monorail or electric *car* / *bike*.
6 We *will* / *won't* need the Internet to talk to people that live far away.

2 06 **Listen to the conversation. Circle the correct answers.**

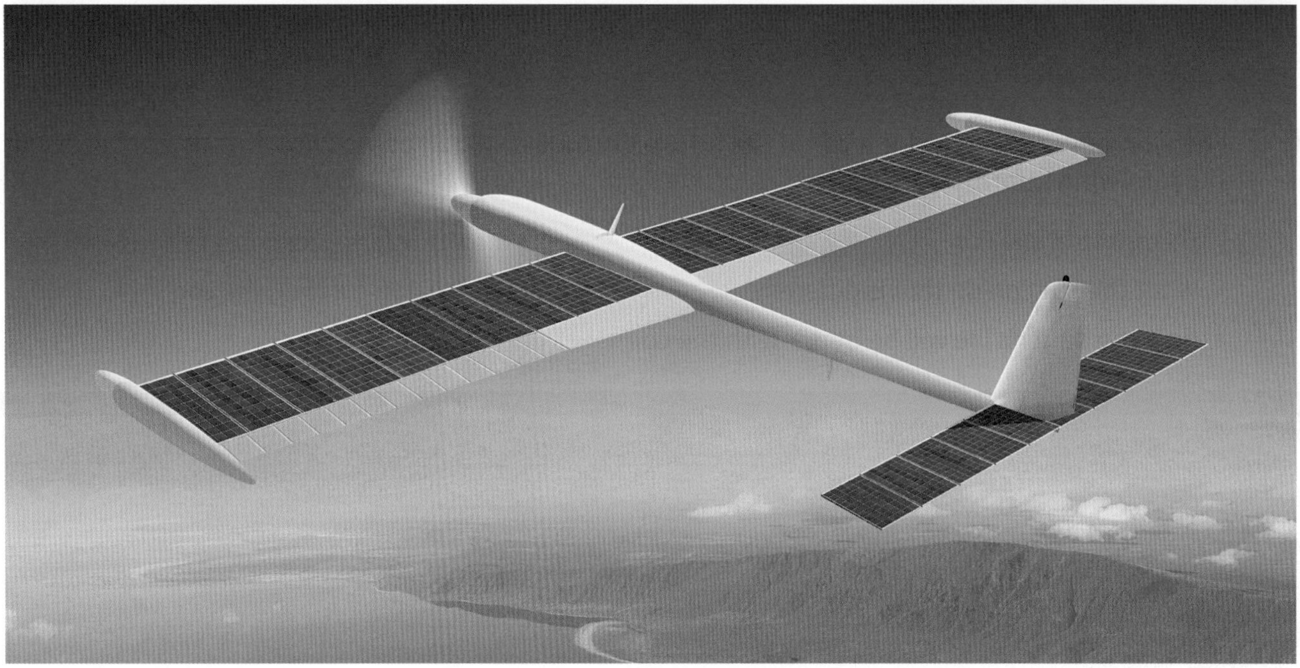

1 Do Leo and Ivy agree with all of the professor's ideas?
  a Yes, they do.
  b No, they don't.
2 Who needs to visit family in Australia?
  a Ivy.
  b Leo.
3 What does Leo think about planes?
  a That people will need them in the future.
  b That people won't need them in the future.
4 Who has read about solar-powered planes?
  a Leo.
  b Ivy.
5 What would Ivy like to use to move around?
  a A cable car.
  b Her birthday present.
6 What did Leo get for his birthday?
  a A microlight.
  b A floating skateboard.

Speaking

1 **Work with a friend. Imagine it is the future. Look at the webpage and choose one vehicle each. Ask and answer the questions about it.**

- What is the vehicle called?
- To use the vehicle, what do you need to do?
- How much is the vehicle?

Get around and have fun!

The Robo-car You don't need to drive to use this car. A robot will drive it for you! You only need to take five lessons on how to use the robot. The Robo-car can be yours for only £250,000.

The JET Z-300 You will love this fantastic jet pack. You just need to press the blue button to fly and the red button to come back down to earth. Easy! For £1,000,000, you can take the JET Z-300 home today.

The Flysurf X Surf the clouds all day with this brilliant flying skateboard! You need to buy a special helmet and take two flying lessons. Then you can travel far and explore the skies! The Flysurf X is only £150,000.

2 **With your friend, agree on a vehicle from Activity 1 that you want to buy together.**

How about buying the Robo-car? I think it will take us to more places in town.

You're right, but I'd like to travel to other cities. I think the JET Z-300 will be quicker.

I'm not sure. The JET Z-300 is really expensive!

3 **Work with another friend. Talk about the vehicle that you chose in Activity 2.**

Nina and I have decided to buy the Flysurf X. It's cheaper than the jet pack. What about you?

3 Past passive

Language focus

Use a **passive sentence** to show interest in who or what is affected by an action, not who or what does the action.

*This tower **was built** hundreds of years ago.*

Also use the passive when it isn't known who did an action.

*The books **were stolen** yesterday afternoon.*

Form the **past passive** with **was** / **were** / **wasn't** / **weren't** + **past participle**. Use the preposition **by** to say who or what did an action when using a passive sentence.

*The Internet **was created** in the 20th century.*

*The first text message **was sent by** a software engineer called Neil Pepworth in 1992.*

Don Quixote ***wasn't written** by William Shakespeare but **by** Miguel de Cervantes.*

*Pyramids **weren't built** in England but they **were built** in Mexico.*

1 Complete the sentences with *was* or *were*.

1 The first email ___was___ sent in 1971.

2 The first telephone call ______ made in 1876.

3 My laptop and smartphone ______ made in China.

4 The rulers of Ancient Egypt ______ called pharaohs.

5 The Eiffel Tower ______ built in Paris.

6 The museum in our town ______ visited by 10,000 people last year.

2 **Circle the correct verbs to complete the dialogue.**

Henry	Would you like to do this quiz?
Catherine	Go on, then.
Henry	All right. Don't look at the screen or you'll see the answers. First one. True or false: the modern Olympic Games (1) *was* / *were* started by Pierre de Coubertin.
Catherine	I know that one. It's true.
Henry	Correct! OK, next one – the pyramids were (2) *built* / *build* by aliens.
Catherine	Oh, come on! That's not a real question. That's false!
Henry	Yes, you're right. Let's move on. Number three – the worldwide web was (3) *created* / *creates* by an American.
Catherine	Yes, I think that's true.
Henry	No, that's false. It was (4) *invent* / *invented* by an Englishman. OK. The Surrealist painter René Magritte *was* / *were* born in France.
Catherine	That's false. Magritte was from Belgium.
Henry	That's right! OK. This is the last one. The 2014 Australian Open tennis tournament was (5) *won* / *win* by Li Na.
Catherine	Oh, I've got no idea. I don't follow tennis. I'll say … true.
Henry	Yes! Well done, Catherine. You got four out of five.

3 **Complete the sentences with the verbs from the box in the correct form.**

win build open hold ~~use~~ give

1 Paper money was first ___used___ in China.
2 The 2016 Olympic Games were ____________ in Brazil.
3 The Blue Mosque in Istanbul was ____________ in the 16th century.
4 The Prado Museum in Madrid was ____________ to the public in 1819.
5 The 2014 football World Cup was ____________ by Germany.
6 The Statue of Liberty was ____________ to the USA by France.

4 **Last night there was a break-in at the New Academy School. Make the sentences passive to describe what happened.**

1 Someone broke the windows. ___The windows were broken.___
2 Someone stole the computers. ____________
3 Someone painted the walls yellow. ____________
4 Someone took all the sports equipment. ____________
5 Someone moved all the desks. ____________
6 Someone threw rubbish in the playground. ____________

a lot of / lots of / a few / a little

Language focus

Use **a lot of** / **lots of** / **a few** / **a little** to talk about the number of people or things.

Use **a lot of** or **lots of** when you want to say that there is a large number.

*There were **a lot of** people at my 12th birthday party.*

Use **a few** with **countable nouns** when you want to say that there is a small number of something.

*I got **a few** bananas from the shop.*

Use **a little** with **uncountable nouns** when you want to say that there is a small amount of something.

*There's only **a little** water left.*

1 Write *a few* or *a little*.

1 <u>a little</u> time
2 ______ books
3 ______ milk
4 ______ bread
5 ______ eggs
6 ______ dogs
7 ______ fruit
8 ______ biscuits
9 ______ bottles
10 ______ people

2 Circle the correct phrases.

1 There were a *lots of* / *lot of* people in the park.
2 I've got *a few* / *a little* books.
3 There were *lots of* / *a few* cars in the car park – we couldn't find anywhere to park.
4 We had *a little* / *lots of* rain – the river flooded.
5 I only made *a lot of* / *a few* mistakes on my Spanish test – I managed to get 95%.
6 My parents have got *a lot of* / *lots* books – over 3,000.

3 Rewrite the sentences by changing the underlined words. Use *a lot of*, *lots of*, *a few* or *a little*.

1 There were only <u>six people</u> in the cinema.
There were only a few people in the cinema.
2 We had <u>ten bottles of milk</u> in the fridge.
______
3 After I finished my homework, I had <u>ten minutes</u> to read before dinner.
______
4 There are <u>20 people</u> in our small swimming pool.
______
5 We've only got <u>three slices</u> of bread. That's not enough.
______
6 I only did <u>one hour of work</u> this afternoon, then I went to the beach!
______

4 What have you got in your bedroom? Write sentences using *a lot of*, *lots of*, *a few* or *a little*.

1 I've got lots of video games.
2 ______
3 ______
4 ______
5 ______
6 ______
7 ______
8 ______

Reading: an informal email

1 **Read the email and answer the questions.**

To jane@worldmail.com

Subject Egypt holiday!

Hi, Aunt Jane

We're back from our holiday in Egypt. We had a really good time, but lots of things went wrong! First, our flight was delayed. We had to stay at the airport for a few hours, waiting to get on the plane. When we finally arrived at our hotel, we weren't given a room with a sea view. The hotel was built 200 years ago and I wanted to tell the manager, 'You need to do some repairs,' but I didn't. Mum and Dad weren't very happy that our rooms weren't cleaned every morning.

Our hotel was near the beach, but there was a big storm on the first day and the beach was closed – it was too dangerous to keep it open. We went to a museum instead and learned about ancient Egyptian pharaohs, tombs and mummies. We bought lots of books on Egypt to take home with us. Unfortunately, I wasn't told until the museum was closing that there was an exhibition on hieroglyphics. We went back the next day, but the exhibition had finished!

The best day was the last day. We left Cairo and went to Giza, where we saw the Sphinx and the pyramids. There were lots of people there. Everyone took lots of photographs.

I hope all is well with you and Uncle Matthew.

Love, Amber

1 What happened at the airport? *The flight was delayed.*
2 How long did they have to wait for their plane at the airport? ________
3 When was the hotel built? ________
4 Why couldn't they go to the beach on the first day? ________
5 Did Amber see the exhibition on hieroglyphics? ________
6 What did they buy lots of at the museum? ________
7 When did they see the Sphinx and the pyramids? ________

Writing

1 **Complete the common phrases used to begin and end informal emails with the words from the box.**

going ~~thanks~~ wait hope forward hear

1 ___Thanks___ for your email.
2 It's great to __________ from you.
3 How's it __________ ?
4 I can't __________ to see you.
5 I'm really looking __________ to seeing you.
6 __________ to hear from you soon.

Help with Writing

The key to writing an email to friends or family members is to use a friendly, informal style.
Use contractions (*I'm* instead of *I am*), use exclamations (!) and write as if you were talking to the person.

2 **Imagine you are Amber's aunt. You and Uncle Matthew had a day trip to London last Saturday. It didn't go very well. Read the information below, then write an email in response to Amber's telling her all about your difficult day trip. Use the phrases from Activity 1.**

- You and Uncle Matthew decided to go to the Ancient Egypt exhibition at the British Museum.
- You went to London by train.
- The train was delayed.
- The exhibition was cancelled.
- On the way home, there were lots of people on the train and not enough seats. You had to stand up.

Listening: pyramids and pharaohs

1 07 **Listen to the conversation. Write *t* (true) or *f* (false).**

1 Milly is reading a book about the Ancient Egyptians. [t]
2 Milly has already finished the book. [ ]
3 Connor has a lot of time to ask Milly some questions. [ ]
4 Milly knows that the pharaohs were buried in pyramids. [ ]
5 Connor answers a question about the pyramids of Giza. [ ]
6 Milly says that slaves had to build the pyramids. [ ]
7 Connor remembers the name for Ancient Egyptian symbols. [ ]

2 08 **Listen and put the story about the pharaoh in order.**

[ ] The pharaoh was taken around in his chariot.
[ ] The pharaoh had to work as a slave for the rest of his life.
[ ] People didn't believe that the pharaoh wasn't a slave.
[1] Every day, the pharaoh was washed and his meals were made.
[ ] The pharaoh changed jobs with his favourite slave.
[ ] The pharaoh was bored with his comfortable life.
[ ] The pharaoh was now a slave. He had to work really hard.

Speaking

1 **Work with a friend. Read the fact file. Then choose your questions and ask and answer.**

Tutankhamun

(c. 1346–1328 BC)

Born: Akhetaten (the capital city of Egypt at that time)

Became pharaoh: c. 1337 BC (when he was nine)

Was pharaoh: c. 1337–1328 BC

Buried: in the Valley of the Kings, in the south of Egypt, west of the Nile River

Famous for: his tomb, which was discovered in 1922 by British archaeologists

Found in his tomb: his mummy, his chariot, clothes, jewellery

Student A

- Where was Tutankhamun born?
- How long was Tutankhamun pharaoh?
- When was Tutankhamun's tomb found?

Student B

- How old was Tutankhamun when he became pharaoh?
- What is Tutankhamun famous for?
- What was there in the pharaoh's tomb?

2 **With your friend, read the fact file in Activity 1 again. Think of and write four more questions about Tutankhamun.**

1 ______________________________

2 ______________________________

3 ______________________________

4 ______________________________

3 **Work with another friend. Ask and answer your questions from Activity 2.**

When was Tutankhamun … ?

He was …

4 could (possibility)

Language focus

Use **could** to talk about an action that is possible now or in the future. After **could**, use the **infinitive without to**.

*We **could win** the Cup this year* not ~~*We could to win the Cup this year.*~~

We often use **could** to make a suggestion about something to do, often in response to a question beginning with **Shall we … ?**

***Shall we** go to the cinema tonight?* *Good idea. We **could see** the new Spider-Man film.*

1 **Are the sentences correct or incorrect? Correct the sentences you think are wrong.**

1 We could has chicken salad for dinner tonight.

Incorrect ___ We could have chicken salad for dinner tonight.

2 We could go to see the match on Sunday.

______ ______

3 Jon's good at playing the guitar. He could joins a band one day.

______ ______

4 If we go to Bilbao, we could visiting the Guggenheim Museum.

______ ______

5 Sue's brilliant at basketball. She could play professionally.

______ ______

6 We could goes to the theatre this weekend. My sister is acting in a play!

______ ______

2 Complete the dialogues with the words from the box.

go watch ideas make ~~shall~~ could

1 Harriet What ___shall___ we do tonight?
Anita We could go to the cinema.
Harriet I'm not keen, to be honest. There's nothing on.

2 Moshin What do you want to do?
Daniel We could ______ swimming.
Moshin Great idea!

3 Toni What shall we do?
Kate We could ______ the football.
Toni Oh, I think it's already started.

4 Cathy What do you want to eat tonight?
Paul We could ______ a pizza.
Cathy OK! Let's go to the supermarket and get what we need.

5 Arturo What shall we do on Saturday?
Bill We ______ stay home and play video games.
Arturo All right. Do you have any good ones?

6 Alina Any ______ ?
Bobby We could watch the gymnastics on TV.
Alina OK. I think it starts in ten minutes' time.

3 Complete the sentences using *could.*

1 Zack enjoys sport and watching TV. He ___could watch the tennis___.
2 Elizabeth's favourite things are exercising and seeing her friends. She ______.
3 Tomas likes meeting new people. He ______.
4 Mila is interested in painting. He ______.
5 Anna enjoys drinking coffee with friends. She ______.
6 Toby loves films. He ______.

Present continuous (future)

Language focus

Use the **present continuous** to talk about something arranged to be done in the future.

*We **aren't visiting** my grandparents on Saturday any more. **We're visiting** them on Sunday instead.*

Although **going to** is also used to talk about personal plans, the present continuous is usually used to be clear that a plan is definite – when it is known when and where something will take place.

I'm going to meet Jay this weekend suggests that the plan is not yet fixed.

I'm meeting Jay at three in the park makes it clear that everything has been arranged.

It is very common to ask someone about their plans by asking them the following question:

What are you doing tonight / tomorrow afternoon / on Saturday?

1 **Use the present continuous to make sentences.**

1 I / meet / cousins / 10 a.m.

I'm meeting my cousins at 10 a.m.

2 We / have / a picnic / on the beach.

____

3 I / see / Tom / at the concert.

____

4 She / play tennis / with Rebecca.

____

5 He / have / a party / for his 13th birthday.

____

6 We / fly back / on Monday morning.

____

2 **Complete the dialogue with *be* and the verbs from the box in the present continuous form.**

have come do meet watch ~~play~~

Jim What are you doing on Saturday, Will?

Will My brother and I (1) are playing in a tennis tournament. What about you?

Jim My grandparents (2) __________ round. It's my mother's birthday. We (3) __________ a big party for her. It's going to be a surprise. Have you done the Science project yet?

Will No, I haven't. I (4) __________ it on Sunday evening after dinner. Dad is going to help me. Have you done it?

Jim Not yet. I (5) __________ Jen and Lucy on Sunday afternoon and we're going to do it together. What are you doing after school tonight?

Will I (6) __________ the match on TV. Do you want to come round?

3 **This is Lucas's diary. Write about his plans.**

Monday	Tuesday	Wednesday	Thursday	Friday	Saturday
Meet Anne, 12 p.m.	Basketball match, 3 p.m.	Film, Saul's house, 6 p.m.	Play chess with Mary at 10 a.m.	Swim with Mary and Saul, 11 a.m.	Picnic, Mum and Dad, 12 p.m.

1 On Monday afternoon he's meeting Anne.
2 On Tuesday afternoon __________
3 On Wednesday afternoon __________
4 On Thursday morning __________
5 On Friday morning __________
6 On Saturday afternoon __________

4 **Now write about your own plans.**

1 What are you doing on Friday evening?

____

2 What are you doing on Saturday morning?

____

3 What are you doing on Saturday afternoon?

____

4 What are you doing on Sunday afternoon?

____

Reading: a leaflet

1 Read the leaflet and write *t* (true) or *f* (false). Correct the false sentences.

The Olympic Sports Camp

at the fantastic Michael Johnson Sports Centre

1st July–31st August

8 a.m.–5 p.m. Monday to Friday

What are you doing this summer? Come along to our exciting Olympic Sports Camp! You could enjoy learning how to do:

Archery Weightlifting Fencing
Gymnastics Boxing

This summer we are also offering a cool new class in how to prepare a healthy diet.

Ages 10–15

Cost: £10 for a four-hour class. Snacks and drinks are all included in the price.

Classes in the morning from 8–12

Classes in the afternoon from 1–5

All of our brilliant sports trainers are fully qualified.

Sign up for sessions before 15th June to get a 20% discount.

For more information, call 612 333.

www.olympicsportscamp.co.uk

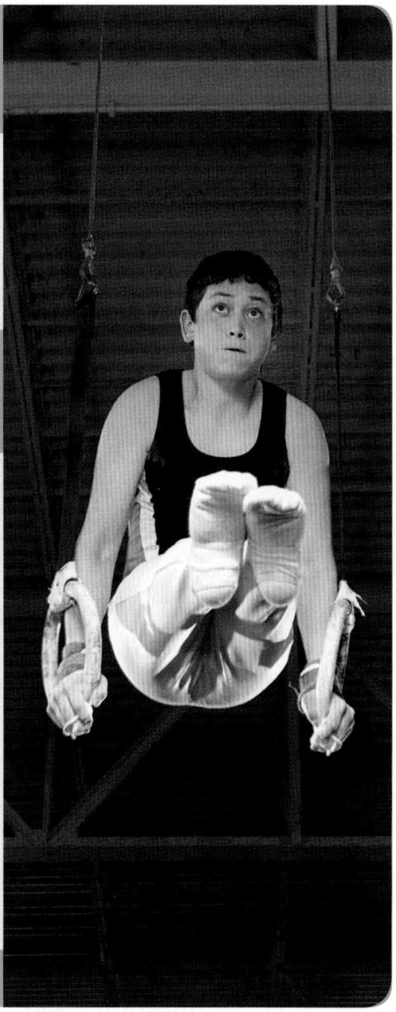

1 The camp offers training in six Olympic sports.
[f] It offers training in five Olympic sports.

2 Last year's camp didn't have a healthy diet class.
[ ] ____________________

3 If you are 12 years old you can go to the camp.
[ ] ____________________

4 A four-hour class costs £12.
[ ] ____________________

5 You have to pay extra for snacks and drinks.
[ ] ____________________

6 You can't get a discount after 15th June.
[ ] ____________________

1 **Complete the sentences with the words from the box.**

information	~~fully qualified~~	learn	included	come	discount	brilliant	class

1 Our trainers are fully qualified.
2 Sign up early to get a ______________.
3 Snacks and drinks are ______________ in the price.
4 Come along to our ______________ Summer Sports Camp.
5 You could ______________ how to do all your favourite sports.
6 Please call for more ______________.
7 We're offering a great new ______________ this year.
8 What's stopping you? ______________ along this summer!

Help with Writing

When creating a leaflet, put what you want to advertise right at the top, use images and make sure that you include contact details such as a phone number and email address.

2 **Design a leaflet for a summer sports camp. Use the sentences from Activity 1. Include the following information:**

- the name of the camp
- the sports people could try at the camp
- a new class you are offering this year
- how much the sessions cost
- how old people have to be to go to the camp.

Listening: time for sport

1 09 Listen. Who suggests the sport? Write *A* (Alex) or *H* (Holly).

1

☐

2

A

3

☐

4

☐

5

☐

6

☐

2 10 Listen and complete Sophie's training schedule with the sports and times.

5.00 p.m.

Day	Sport	Time
Monday	swimming	5 p.m.
Tuesday		
Wednesday		
Thursday		

Speaking

1 **Work with a friend. Read about the sports centre. Then choose your questions and ask and answer.**

The *Extreme* Sports Centre

Are you good at sports? Would you like to try a new one? At the Extreme Sports Centre, you can do sporting activities while having an exciting time!

Try these sports:

climbing — bungee jumping

skateboarding — BMX biking

Price:

£5 for one hour

£9 for two hours

£12 for three hours

Our opening times are:

Tuesday to Friday: 4 p.m. to 8 p.m.

Saturday and Sunday: 11 a.m. to 8 p.m.

Student A

- What sports can you do at the centre?
- Is the sports centre open on Mondays?

Student B

- How much does it cost?
- Can you go there at the weekend?

Help with Speaking

When you and a friend have to choose something, you have to try to agree. Make suggestions, and listen to your friend's ideas. Don't forget to respond with, for example, *Good idea!*, *That sounds great!*, *I'm not sure …*, *I don't think …*, etc.

2 **With your friend, choose one extreme sport to try. Agree on:**

- the sport
- the day and time to try it
- how long you would like to do the sport.

We could try bungee jumping.

I'm not sure. I'm afraid of jumping. What about BMX biking?

Good idea! We could go on Sunday at 11.30.

OK! And we could try it for one hour.

3 **Work with another friend. Tell them about your plans from Activity 2.**

Grace and I are going to try BMX biking at the Extreme Sports Centre. We're going on Sunday at 11.30. We're going for one hour.

5 Present perfect with *ever / never*

Language focus

Use the **present perfect** to talk about things that happened in the past without having to be clear about when the action happened.

*My sister **has lived** in Italy* not ~~*My sister has lived in Italy three years ago.*~~

Form the present perfect with **has** / **have** + **past participle**. In informal spoken and written English, the contracted form is usually used.

Full form	Contracted form
*He **has read** lots of books about London.*	*He**'s read** lots of books about London.*

Use the **present perfect** with **ever** / **never** to talk about things that you have or haven't done. **Ever** means 'at any time in your life up to now'. Questions beginning with **Have you ever** are a common way of asking someone about the experiences they have had.

***Have you ever** met a famous person?* *Yes, I have. / No, I haven't.*

Never means 'not ever' or 'at no time in your life up to now'. Use the word with an affirmative rather than a negative verb.

*I have **never** met a famous person* not ~~*I haven't never met a famous person.*~~

1 Complete the sentences with *ever* or *never*.

1 My brother has ___never___ played the piano.
2 Have you __________ written a story?
3 You've __________ been to London? Really? I'm very surprised.
4 I've __________ been to Moscow, but I'd like to go there one day.
5 I've watched the Star Wars films many times, but my brother has __________ seen them.
6 Have you __________ tried Japanese food?

2 Write the past participles.

1 make ___made___
2 see ______
3 swim ______
4 do ______
5 eat ______
6 ride ______
7 win ______
8 cook ______
9 build ______
10 buy ______

3 Complete the questions with the verbs from Activity 2.

1 Have you ever ___made___ a pancake?
2 Have any of your friends ever ______ a competition?
3 Have you ever ______ a tree house?
4 Has your sister ever ______ Polish food?
5 Have you ever ______ in the Pacific Ocean?
6 Have you ever ______ a horse?
7 Have you ever ______ a crossword puzzle?
8 Has your brother ever ______ a meal for the whole family?
9 Have you ever ______ a computer?
10 Have your parents ever ______ a film in English?

4 Match the questions from Activity 3 with answers a–j.

a No, I haven't. They're too expensive. ______
b Yes, he has. Many times. He's the chef of the family. ______
c Yes, I have. My brother and I built one with my dad when we were young. ______
d I'm not sure. I'll have to ask them when I see them at school. ______
e No, I haven't, but my mother has. She loves doing them. ______
f Yes, they have. They love watching films in other languages. ______
g No, I haven't. I think I'd fall off. ______
h Yes, I have. Once, two summers ago. It was very warm. ______
i Yes, she has. She lives in Warsaw! ______
j Yes, I have. They are my favourite things to make! ___1___

Present perfect with past simple detail

Language focus

Use the **present perfect** to talk about experiences. Begin a conversation about someone's experiences by asking them a present perfect question with **ever**.

*Have you **ever** tried snowboarding?*

Answer these kinds of questions with **Yes, I have** or **No, I haven't**. To tell someone more about an experience, use the **past simple**.

*Yes, I have! I **tried** it once, a long time ago, when I **was** on holiday in Canada.*

Further questions can then be asked using the past simple.

Did you like it? — *No, I didn't. I wasn't very good at it.*

Where did you stay in Canada? — *In Banff, in the Rocky Mountains. We really liked it there.*

1 **Complete the table.**

Infinitive	Past simple	Past participle
drive	drove	driven
find		found
sing		
sleep	slept	
	broke	
drink		drunk

2 Complete the dialogues with the verbs from Activity 1.

1 Have you ever ___sung___ a song in front of an audience?
Yes, I have. Last month, I ________ songs from *Les Misérables* to 300 people at my school.

2 Have you ever ________ tomato juice?
Yes, I have. I ________ some at my grandmother's birthday party without knowing what it was. It was horrible!

3 Have you ever ________ outside?
Yes, I have. My sister and I ________ in a tent last summer when it was really hot.

4 Have you ever ________ across the USA in a Cadillac?
Yes, I have. My mum ________ my brother and me from Los Angeles to New York two years ago.

5 Have you ever ________ something valuable?
No, I haven't, but my friend ________ a gold watch on the street outside my house a few weeks ago.

6 Have your ever ________ your leg?
No, I haven't, but I ________ my left arm when I was six years old.

3 Complete the questions with *has* / *have* and the verbs from the box.

be (x2) read live upload ~~see~~

1 ___Have___ you ever ___seen___ a play?
2 ________ your brother ever ________ to Guatemala?
3 ________ your mum ever ________ on TV?
4 ________ your sister ever ________ in another country?
5 ________ you ever ________ a video to the Internet?
6 ________ your dad ever ________ a book in French?

4 Match the questions from Activity 3 with answers a–f.

a Yes, he has. He read *Le Petit Prince.* ____
b Yes, I have. Last year we saw a brilliant one about medieval London. __1__
c Yes, I have. Yesterday afternoon – it was my guide to learning the guitar. ____
d No, she hasn't, but she would like to live in Australia. ____
e No, she hasn't, but Dad was on the news once. ____
f Yes, he has. He lived in Mexico for five years and then he travelled all around the Americas. ____

Reading: a book review

1 **Read the review. Answer the questions.**

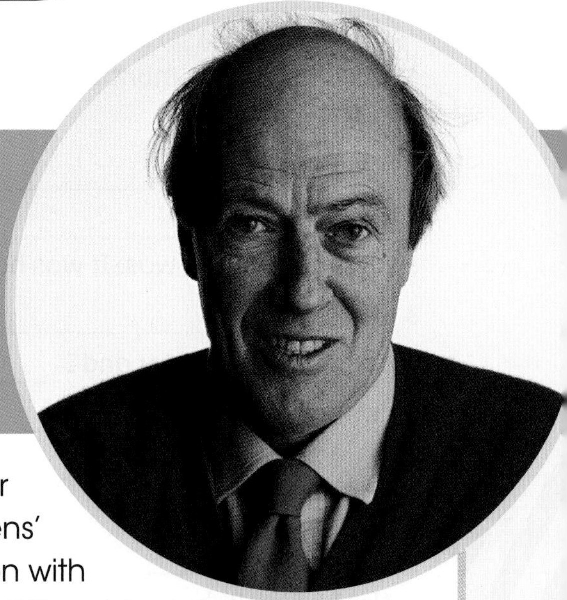

A Giant in Buckingham Palace

by Amanda Neil

I have read many stories set in London – the Paddington Bear books, *Mary Poppins*, *Peter Pan*. I've even read Charles Dickens' *Oliver Twist*, as well as lots of his other tales of Victorian London with their strange and interesting characters going in and out of all the old shops of the city – the tailor's, the baker's, the jeweller's, the barber's. But the best book set in London that I have ever read is Roald Dahl's *The BFG*. I first read it when I was eight years old. I have enjoyed it several times since then; the last time was just the other day. Have you ever read it? No? What, never? Stop what you're doing and read it now!

The BFG was first published in 1982 and has been popular with readers ever since. It tells the story of a character called the Big Friendly Giant (the BFG of the title) and the friendship that he has with an orphan girl called Sophie. Together, Sophie and the BFG have to stop the other giants, all of whom are horrible, from eating children. The pair end up going all the way to Buckingham Palace in London to get the Queen to help them.

What I most enjoy about this book is the language. The BFG uses funny, invented words such as 'snozzcumber', 'gobblefunking' and 'whizzpopping'. Dahl's character is like a perfect uncle or grandad, with a wonderful imagination, a big heart and a sense of adventure. I recommend *The BFG* to anyone who likes being silly with words and enjoys a good story, and especially to those readers who want to be taken deep into the world of dreams.

1. Has the writer read any books by Charles Dickens? Yes, she has.
2. How many times has the writer read *The BFG*? ______
3. Who wrote *The BFG*? ______
4. When was *The BFG* first published? ______
5. Name two characters from *The BFG*. ______
6. What aspect of the book does the writer like the most? ______

1 **Complete the text with the words from the box.**

critics recommendation story ~~reviews~~ opinion information

Introduction to Book Reviewing

People who write book (1) ___reviews___ are called reviewers or (2) ________. A review has four main purposes: to give (3) ________ about a book (the title, the name of the author); to describe the (4) ________ (but not say exactly what happens); to give your (5) ________ (if you think it is good or not); and to give a (6) ________ – for example, *You should read this book* or *I don't recommend this book.*

Help with Writing

When you write a review of a book, don't give away all the details of its plot. You should give readers a sense of the story rather than tell them everything that happens in it.

2 **Write a review of a book you have read recently. Include the following information:**

- the title of the book
- the author's name
- what the book is about
- what you think of the book
- your recommendation.

Listening: city experiences

1 11 **Listen and answer the questions.**

1 Has anyone in the class ever been to New York?
Yes, Jane has been to New York.
2 Why did Jacob enjoy being in Rome?
____
3 How many times has Miss Collins visited Cairo?
____
4 Has Carmen ever been to Cairo?
____
5 Who lives in London?
____
6 How long was Carmen in London?
____

2 12 **Listen to the conversation. Circle the correct answers.**

1 How long did Max stay in London?
a All summer.
(b) A week.

2 Who did Max go to visit?
a His dad.
b His aunt.

3 What did Max enjoy the most?
a A film.
b The parks in London.

4 Does Emma know about the Great Fire of London?
a Yes, she does.
b No, she doesn't.

5 Which shops did the film show?
a A chemist's, a tailor's, a carpenter's and a baker's.
b A chemist's, a tailor's and a carpenter's.

6 What did the cinema room smell like?
a It smelt like London in 1666.
b It smelt like the London streets today.

Speaking

1 **Work with a friend. Talk about the shops. Ask and answer.**

Have you ever been to a chemist's?

Yes, I have. I went there a long time ago with my mum.

What did you do or buy?

We bought some sun cream.

2 **With your friend, talk about going to one of the shops in Activity 1. Agree on five things to buy or do there.**

Let's go to the baker's. We could buy some nice bread.

Good idea. Let's get some chocolate biscuits, too.

3 **Work with another friend. Tell them what you have bought from the shop in Activity 2.**

Charlie and I have been to the baker's. We've bought some bread, some chocolate biscuits, a packet of …

6 too many / not enough

Language focus

Use ***too many*** / ***not enough*** to talk about how much there is of something.

Use **too many** to say that there is more of something countable than you need.

Use **not enough** to say that there is not as much of something as you need.

*My brother's got **too many** video games. He doesn**'t** have **enough** time to play them all.*

1 **Complete the sentences with *too*, *many* or *enough*.**

1 There were too ___many___ people on the bus. I had to stand up.
2 I didn't buy ______________ milk when I went to the supermarket.
3 There are ______________ many people on the London Underground.
4 Mum says she hasn't got ______________ time to do everything.
5 I didn't have ______________ money to buy the computer game.
6 I've got too ______________ things to do today.
7 Dad's got too ______________ CDs. They're all over the house!
8 My brother owns too ______________ guitars. Last week he bought his fifth!

2 Circle the correct phrases.

1 *We haven't got enough* / *We've got too many* time! We'll never get to the train station by 5 o'clock.
2 *There are too many* / *There aren't enough* smartphones in the world. No one wants to talk any more; they just want to look at their screens.
3 *She didn't have enough* / *She had too many* coins with her. She couldn't afford to get a bottle of water from the machine.
4 *There are too many* / *There aren't enough* hours in the day! How can we get everything done?
5 *We bought too many* / *We didn't buy enough* potatoes. We don't need this many for a roast dinner. Let's save some for tomorrow.
6 *I've not got enough* / *I've got too many* pairs of shoes. I don't need them all.

3 Rewrite the sentences with *too many* or *not enough* and a suitable noun.

1 We've only got two chairs. We need four.
We haven't got enough chairs.
2 We've only got one loaf of bread. We need three.
____
3 We've got six big packets of crisps. We only need two.
____
4 We've got three chocolate cakes. We only need one.
____
5 We've only got one bottle of water. We need three.
____
6 We've got three packets of biscuits. We only need one.
____

4 What have you got too many of or not enough of? Write sentences.

1 ______________________________
2 ______________________________
3 ______________________________
4 ______________________________
5 ______________________________

Can you tell me what this is / does / is for?

Language focus

Use **Can you tell me what this is / does / is for?** to ask someone to explain the function of something.

Can you tell me what this *button* ***is for?***

Questions beginning with **Can you tell me … ?** are a less direct and more polite way of asking someone something.

1 **Choose the correct words to complete the dialogues.**

1 Can you tell me what a screwdriver *do* / *is for*?
It's for turning screws.

2 Can you tell me what *is for* / *this is*?
It's a spanner. It's for holding and turning nuts.

3 Can you tell me what a drill is *for* / *this is*?
It's for making holes.

4 Can you tell me what this machine *does* / *do*?
It makes yoghurt.

5 Can you tell me what a lever *this is* / *does*?
It operates a machine.

6 Can you tell me what a saw *for* / *is for*?
It's for cutting wood.

2 Complete the questions with the words from the box.

tell me for ~~you~~ does is

1 Can ___you___ tell me what this is?
2 Can you tell me what this tool ________ for?
3 Can you tell me what this lever is ________?
4 Can you tell me what this machine ________?
5 Can you tell ________ what this switch is for?
6 Can you ________ me what this button is for?

3 Match questions 1–6 in Activity 2 with answers a–f.

a It's just a light switch. It's for turning the light on and off. Nothing special. ____
b This lever is for starting that machine. ____
c It translates things perfectly. It's a language machine. ____
d This? No, I can't tell you anything about it. It's top secret. __1__
e This tool is very special. It's for, um … Do you know, I can't remember. ____
f Oh, this button is for increasing the temperature in the building. ____

4 Complete the questions with *do*, *does* or *for*.

1 Can you tell me what this is ___for___? It's for making bread.
2 Can you tell me what this machine is ________? It's for heating liquids.
3 Can you tell me what this machine ________? It cleans tools.
4 Can you tell me what these machines ________? They regulate the temperature.
5 Can you tell me what this ________? It cuts cheese into blocks.
6 Can you tell me what this is ________? It's for keeping things clean.
7 Can you tell me what these ________? They hold everything in place.
8 Can you tell me what this is ________? It's for mixing chemicals.

Reading: a blog post

1 **Read the blog post and write *t* (true) or *f* (false). Correct the false sentences.**

My Blog World

Welcome to My Blog World again. What I want to talk about today is time. I just haven't got enough of it. I'm sure you know what I mean. There are too many things to do, aren't there? Every day I spend ages answering my little sister's questions. 'Arthur,' she says, 'can you tell me what this lever is for? Can you tell me what this button does? Can you tell me what happens when you press this switch?' (Yes, I think she is going to be a scientist.) I want to say, 'Go away!' but I am not an unkind boy. After I have answered all of Beth's questions, I feel tired and need to sit down.

Beth is not the only reason I don't have enough time. School takes up too much of my day. I've got too many tests to do and not enough time to study for them all. Another thing – I love reading, but there are far too many books to read. I'm interested in everything, you see, especially how things are made. Every time I see an interesting new book I really want to read it. It could be about Albert Einstein's life, the greatest inventors of all time or the history of the aircraft engine, but my 'Books I Really Want To Read' list is getting longer and longer and I sometimes think that instead of reading any of these books, all I will ever do is make a note of their titles.

What can I do? Mum always says, 'Arthur, you're writing far too many blog posts. You won't have enough time for your inventions. Perhaps you should stop writing them.' Hmm. Maybe she's right. She usually is. Then again, maybe what I actually need to do is invent some extra time. Now that's an interesting idea!

1 Arthur finds the time to do everything he wants to do.

[f] He hasn't got enough time to do everything he wants to do.

2 Arthur's sister doesn't ask him any questions.

[ ] ______

3 Arthur doesn't say 'go away' to his sister.

[ ] ______

4 Arthur has got too many tests to do at school.

[ ] ______

5 Arthur doesn't have many interests.

[ ] ______

6 Arthur doesn't think his mother's idea is a good one.

[ ] ______

Writing

1 **Match 1–5 with a–e to make ways of beginning a blog post about time.**

1	What I want to	a	to talk about today.	____
2	I'd like to	b	my mind today is time.	____
3	The thing that is on	c	talk about today is time.	1
4	Today's post is all	d	about time.	____
5	Time is what I want	e	talk about time	____

Help with Writing

The best blogs are written by people who write about things that really interest them. Blogs are a kind of public diary, a way of telling the world who you are. When you write a blog, be open and honest about your interests and feelings.

2 **Write a blog post about not having enough time to do things. Begin your blog post with one of the phrases from Activity 1. Include the following information:**

- the name of your blog
- why you don't have enough time (e.g. you've got too many things to do around the house)
- what you would like to change and how you would change it.

Listening: inventors and inventions

1 13 **Listen to the story. Complete the sentences.**

1 One of Cynthia's inventions is a flying car.
2 Molly would like to become an ________ in the future.
3 Cynthia's laboratory was untidy. There were too many ________ ________ on the floor.
4 The screwdrivers and spanners were on a long ________.
5 There were some ________ and ________ on a big table.
6 One assistant had a ________ in their hand and the other one had a paintbrush.
7 Cynthia pressed a ________ on the wall to turn off the lights.
8 Cynthia's next invention will be a ________ to keep toast warm.

2 14 **Listen to the conversation. Answer the questions.**

1 How long has Molly been at Cynthia's laboratory?
She's been there for six hours.
2 What is the big grey machine?
____
3 What is the red switch for?
____
4 Which object does the yellow lever move?
____
5 Which tools did Cynthia learn to use with her mum?
____
6 What does Molly like doing?
____
7 Which two things are needed for a good invention?
____

Speaking

1 Work with a friend. Look at these great inventions. Play the guessing game.

Can you tell me what it does?

It tells the time.

Can you tell me what it's for?

It's for keeping food cold.

1 the clock

2 the wheel

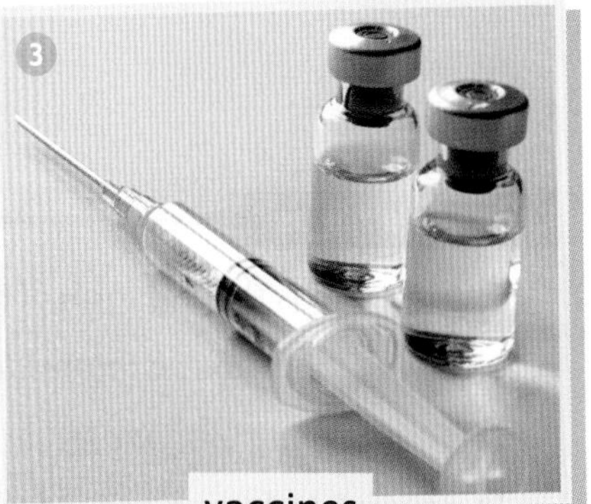
3 vaccines

4 the fridge

5 the light bulb

6 the Internet

2 With your friend, talk about the inventions in Activity 1. Why are they important? Say one idea each.

The wheel is important because it helps us travel more quickly.

Yes. It also helps us move things easily from one place to another.

3 Think of another great invention. Say why it is important.

I think video games are a great invention. They can help you relax and have fun with your friends after working hard!

7 Gerunds

Language focus

The **gerund** is the **ing** form of a verb. Use the gerund as a noun.

***Learning** languages is interesting.*

*I enjoy **learning** languages.*

In general, to form a gerund, add **ing** to the infinitive: **do** **doing**

If the verb ends in a single **e**, cut the **e** before writing **ing**: **have** **having**

Be is an exception. The gerund is **being** not ~~**bing**~~.

If the verb ends with a consonant–vowel–consonant pattern, double the final consonant, then add **ing**: **swim** **swimming**

Don't double the letter **y** – for example, the gerund of **buy** is **buying** not ~~**buyying**~~.

1 Put the words in the correct order to make sentences.

1 is / fun / cooking / good / .

Cooking is good fun.

2 us / tired / makes / late / bed / going / to / .

____

3 is / new / exciting / learning / things / .

____

4 idea / every / a good / isn't / eating / day / chocolate / .

____

5 your / dangerous / a helmet / riding / without / is / bike / .

____

6 bad for / in / your feet / footwear / is / running / wrong / the / .

____

2 Write the gerunds.

1 swim swimming
2 live ______
3 get ______
4 travel ______
5 study ______
6 make ______
7 come ______
8 play ______
9 go ______
10 write ______
11 see ______
12 watch ______

3 Complete the sentences with gerunds from Activity 2.

1 Swimming in the sea is more enjoyable than in a pool.
2 ______ to the cinema is always lots of fun.
3 ______ hard for exams can be difficult, but it's worth it.
4 ______ a good night's sleep is very important.
5 ______ friends in a new school isn't easy.
6 ______ the world by train, bus, boat and plane – that is my mother's dream.

4 Complete the sentences with a gerund.

1 Doing homework is really boring.
2 ______ books is a great way to learn about the world.
3 ______ is my favourite thing to do. Sometimes my alarm clock doesn't wake me up!
4 ______ the guitar is my sister's favourite thing to do – she does it morning, noon and night. She's so noisy! She's quite good at it, though.
5 ______ on holiday is great fun. I love seeing new places and having a break from being at home and school.
6 ______ a foreign language is interesting, but it isn't easy. You have to practise a lot: speaking, reading, writing, listening – everything!
7 ______ lots of time with my friends is very important to me.
8 ______ a big house isn't important in life.

Reported speech

Language focus

Use **reported speech** to tell someone what another person said.

Chen said that ***she came from Hong Kong.***

In reported speech there are some changes to the grammar of the sentence. The basic idea is that what is in the present in direct speech is in the past in reported speech.

Direct speech	Reported speech
I'm tired.	*My brother said that* ***he was tired****.*
I'm not going to the party.	*Mirko said that* ***he wasn't going to the party****.*

Notice how the pronouns and determiners change from direct to reported speech.

You *have to study for* ***your*** *test.*	*Mum said that* ***I*** *had to study for* ***my*** *test.*

The conjunction **that** is used in reported speech, but it can be left out.

Sally said ***that*** *she passed all of her exams* or *Sally said she passed all of her exams.*

1 Complete the sentences with the verbs from the box in the correct form.

be play like want ~~listen~~ not want

1 He said that he ___listened___ to music every day.
2 We said we ____________ the new English teacher.
3 She said that she ____________ anything to drink because she wasn't thirsty.
4 They said that they ____________ football in the park every Saturday morning.
5 You said you ____________ to go to the cinema.
6 I said that I ____________ from Russia.

2 Circle the correct verbs forms.

1 We need some milk.
He said that they (need) some milk. a needing (b) needed

2 I don't enjoy watching sport on the TV.
He said that he (not enjoy) watching sport on the TV. a didn't enjoy b hasn't enjoyed

3 I have to go to bed.
He said that he (have) to go to bed. a had b having

4 We're going now.
They said that they (go) now. a went b were going

5 I'm watching a film.
She said that she (watch) a film. a was watching b watched

6 This is a brilliant game.
She said that it (be) a brilliant game. a was b were

3 Change the reported speech to direct speech.

1 Millie said that she didn't like watching TV.
I don't like watching TV.

2 Carl said that he was reading an interesting book.
___

3 Tanya said that she enjoyed writing stories.
___

4 Iain said that he wanted to go to the cinema.
___

5 Brigit said that she was from the USA.
___

4 Change the direct speech to reported speech using *that*.

1 I love video games.
Martin said that he loved video games.

2 I can't do the Maths homework.
Robert said ___

3 My favourite food is spaghetti.
Carly said ___

4 I'm having a great time!
Lola said ___

5 I don't understand.
Mia said ___

Reading: a travel diary

1 **Read the travel diary. Complete the table.**

The diary of an astronaut

Day 3 Space! I can't believe it. Here I am on the great mission – the Voyage to Mars. We're going to be on board a long, long time. We're all very excited. Jane Markham, our commander, said that being in space for the first time was the best moment of her life. I feel the same. It was my childhood dream – and now it's real!

Day 41 Everything takes so long in zero gravity! Going to the toilet – ugh! Don't talk about it! But Samuel Conrad, who is our chief engineer, said that floating around inside the spaceship is great fun. He's right. It is!

Day 62 The food – hmm. It's like being stuck on an aeroplane. It's not great, but we're all getting used to it. The most important thing is to hold on to it or it will float away!

Day 171 Going into space must be very interesting, one of my fans wrote to me in an email. Yes, it is. I am a very lucky man. Alma Black (she is the youngest member of the crew and our expert on the computer systems) said this morning that her life was like a science-fiction film.

Day 331 Looking back at Earth from space is an amazing thing to do. In fact, it is my favourite thing to do from space – our world looks so beautiful from up here. But I don't like the sunrises. We see them every 90 minutes – about 16 a day! I would rather see only one.

Day 427 Walking down the street, lying on my back in the garden on a sunny day, breathing fresh air – how I would love to do those things now that I can't do them! After more than a year on board, we're all beginning to want more room to move. There are 1,267 days left before we return home.

Name of the mission	Voyage to Mars
Number of astronauts mentioned in the diary	
Things the astronaut likes in space	
Things the astronaut doesn't like in space	
Things the astronaut misses about life on Earth	

1 Answer the questions.

1 What do you think would be the best thing about being in space?

____

2 What do you think would be the worst thing about being in space?

____

3 What do you think astronauts miss about life on Earth?

____

4 What do you think astronauts don't miss about life on Earth?

____

Help with Writing

When you write an entry in a travel diary, make a note of the date and your location: *6 p.m., Monday 12 July, outside the Leaning Tower of Pisa.* / *Saturday morning, 3 October, in a café in Moscow.*

2 Imagine you are an astronaut. You are on the first mission to Mars. Write a travel diary about your journey to the red planet. Include the following information:

- what you do on the spaceship
- how you feel
- what you miss about life at home
- what you find most interesting about being in space.

Listening: space

1 15 **Listen and write *James* or *Dad*.**

1 James likes going to museums.
2 ______ thinks that a lunar module is uncomfortable.
3 ______ finds a countdown clock in the museum.
4 ______ sees a spacesuit next to some photos of the moon.
5 For ______, wearing a spacesuit would be amazing.
6 ______ wouldn't like to be an astronaut.
7 ______ is tired after walking around the museum.
8 ______ suggests having 'space sandwiches' for lunch.

2 16 **Listen to the conversation. Write *t* (true) or *f* (false).**

1 Helen's brother said that he saw an alien in his dream. [t]
2 He said that when he was at the lake, a space capsule landed. [ ]
3 He said that a little green alien came out of the capsule. [ ]
4 He said that the alien had yellow spots on her hands and feet. [ ]
5 He said that the alien touched his dog, and that she was nice. [ ]
6 He said that at that point in the dream, he woke up. [ ]

Speaking

1 Work with a friend. Read the ideas. Do you agree or disagree? Say why.

I don't think taking animals into space is a good idea. They can get hurt or ill.

I agree. Animals were born to live on Earth!

1 Going into space with animals is a good idea.

2 We don't need another mission to the moon.

3 Discovering aliens is the most important reason to go into space.

4 Space travel is bad for the environment.

5 Thanks to space travel, we have learned a lot about our planet.

Help with Speaking

When you give an opinion, you can use *I think* or *I don't think*. You can give the same opinion using one phrase or the other. Look at these examples:
*I **think** taking animals into space is a **bad** idea.*
*I **don't think** taking animals into space is a **good** idea.*

2 Think of and write three more ideas about space. Use the topics in the box or other topics.

rockets and the environment
studying our solar system
holidays on the moon
building more spaceships than planes

1 ______________________
2 ______________________
3 ______________________

3 Work with another friend. Share your ideas from Activity 2. Say if you agree or disagree.

I think rockets pollute the environment. Engineers should stop making them.

I don't agree. I think …

8 Question tags with *be*

Language focus

Use **question tags** with **be** to check information or to find out if the person you are speaking to agrees with you about something.

If the verb in the sentence is positive, the verb in the question tag is negative.

*You'**re** from Ankara, **aren't** you?*

If the verb in the sentence is negative, the verb in the question tag is positive.

*The weather **isn't** very nice, **is** it?*

Put a comma before the question tag and use contractions with a negative form of **be**.

*It's cold, **isn't it**?* not ~~*It's cold, is not it?*~~

1 **Complete the questions.**

1 The North Pole ____*is*____ one of the coldest places on Earth, isn't it?
2 Penguins ________ big, aren't they?
3 Female seals ________ bigger than male seals, are they?
4 A sledge ________ for sleeping on, is it?
5 He ________ knitting some mittens, isn't he?
6 Whales ________ mammals, aren't they?

2 Circle the correct answers.

1 Tom's a great swimmer, *is he* / *isn't he* ?

2 Burak isn't coming to watch the film about polar bears on Saturday, *isn't he* / *is he* ?

3 You're not reading that book about icebergs, *are you* / *aren't you* ?

4 It's hot today, *isn't it* / *is it* ?

5 You're interested in life in the Arctic, *are you* / *aren't you* ?

6 Your sister is good at Science, *isn't she* / *is she* ?

3 Use question tags to complete the sentences.

1 The Northern Lights are beautiful, aren't they?

2 Polar bears aren't black, ______________

3 Igloos are made of ice, ______________

4 The North Pole isn't colder than the South Pole, ______________

5 You're drawing a picture of a seal, ______________

6 Penguins aren't able to fly, ______________

4 Correct the question tags.

1 The climate is changing in the Arctic, is it? isn't it?

2 Ice floes are sheets of floating ice, isn't they? ______________

3 We're sailing to the North Pole, are we? ______________

4 She's studying the Arctic, aren't she? ______________

5 We aren't learning about glaciers today, aren't we? ______________

6 He's watching a film about mammoths, is he? ______________

7 You aren't interested in icebergs, aren't you? ______________

8 Glaciers aren't getting smaller, are it? ______________

may / might

Language focus

Use **may** / **might** to talk about an action that is possible now or in the future.

*We **might** win this match.*

After **may** and **might**, use the **infinitive without to**.

*We **may** go to Venice this summer* not ~~*We may to go to Venice this summer*~~.

May and **might** are often used similarly to **could**.

*It **may** / **might** / **could** rain later.*

However, notice the difference between them.

*We **could** watch the new Star Wars film.*
(Watching the Star Wars film is one of the many things that it is possible for us to do.)

*We **might** see the new Spider-Man film.*
(It is possible but not certain that we will do it.)

1 Complete the sentences with the verbs from the box.

start have go want be ~~enter~~

1 I may not ___enter___ the chess tournament.
2 Miss Smith says we may __________ another History test next week.
3 Carrie says she may __________ writing a blog.
4 I may not __________ to the party tomorrow. I've got too much homework to do.
5 Andreas might not __________ to watch it. He doesn't like fantasy films.
6 It may __________ hot at the weekend. If it is, let's go to the beach.

2 Match 1–6 with a–f.

1 We may not play tennis this afternoon.
2 I might meet Julia tonight.
3 My friends may go to the beach on Sunday.
4 My sister might not go to university in the UK.
5 Our team might win this year.
6 It may snow at the weekend.

a That's what it said on the weather forecast. ____
b I'll join them if I finish my English project. ____
c I think we're good enough. ____
d She may go somewhere in the USA instead. ____
e She's back from Galicia. ____
f Mum said it might rain. 1

3 Are the sentences correct or incorrect? Correct the sentences you think are wrong.

1 It might being really cold at the weekend.
Incorrect It might be really cold at the weekend.

2 Helen might not want anything to eat.
____ ____

3 Sam says he may to come to the party on Saturday.
____ ____

4 We may spend a week in Lisbon in the summer.
____ ____

5 I might gone to the cinema tomorrow afternoon.
____ ____

6 The polar ice caps might melting.
____ ____

4 Circle the correct forms of *may* and *might*.

1 My weather app says there ____ be a storm coming. Let's go inside!
(a) may b may not

2 Boris ____ come to the park on Sunday. His grandparents are visiting.
a might not b might

3 We ____ have a picnic tomorrow. Would you like to come?
a may not b may

4 Cristina ____ be uploading some of her songs to YouTube later. She said she wants to share her new material.
a might b might not

5 We ____ go to the pool tomorrow. Everyone wants to go on the new slide!
a might b might not

6 Rana ____ know about the concert. Let's text him and tell him all about it!
a might not b might

Reading: a story

1 **Read the story and order the events.**

This isn't a story, is it?

Yesterday was a most unusual day. Wherever Richard the penguin went, he was asked questions. He was cycling along an ice floe, on his way to his traditional Saturday-morning visit to the igloo library, when a seal shouted out, 'You're Richard, aren't you? My brother is in your How To Watch Out For Polar Bears class!'

Later, Richard was by himself at the library, and, as he was looking at the books about human beings and their ways, a seal pup appeared at his side. She said, 'You're quite tall, aren't you? Would you get *How To Fly* down from the top shelf for me, please?'

In the supermarket, where Richard went for some fish cereal, other penguins kept saying, 'It's hotter than normal today, isn't it?' or 'This weather is great, isn't it?' Richard didn't think it was great because he was very concerned about global warming, but he didn't say anything.

By the time Richard got home, he was wondering why people seemed so keen on asking him things. He had no idea. Just then, his dad came in from the large chunk of ice he had been sitting on and said, 'Hi, Richard. You aren't hungry, are you? If you are, I'll make us some fish soup and we can chat about the day. Now, if you're lucky, I may have some prawns in here.' It was only when Richard was in his bedroom that night, and undressing before going to sleep, that he realised that the sentence on his T-shirt read, 'You're asking me a question, aren't you?'

a A seal pup asks Richard to help her. ____
b Richard's dad says he will make something to eat. ____
c Richard begins cycling to the library. 1
d Richard meets a seal pup. ____
e Richard goes to the supermarket. ____
f Richard sees the sentence on his T-shirt. ____

1 **Complete these sentences from the story with the phrases from the box. Then look back at the story to check your answers.**

Richard was by himself at the library	his dad came in	
Richard was in his bedroom that night	Richard got home	~~was a most unusual day~~

1 Yesterday was a most unusual day ________.

2 Later, ________.

3 By the time ________.

4 Just then, ________.

5 It was only when ________.

Help with Writing

If the reader knows when a story took place, i.e. *yesterday, last week, many years ago*, it is easier for them to make sense of it. It is also a good idea to order the sequence of events in the story. You can do this by using time expressions such as *then, afterwards, after that, at that moment, suddenly, a moment later* and *later on*.

2 **You are going to write a short story about something unusual that happened at the North Pole. Use time expressions in your story. Before you write your story, plan it by making notes about the following:**

- the title of the story
- the plot (what happens in the story)
- the characters (the people or animals in the story).

Listening: to the Arctic

1 17 **Listen to the conversation. Circle the correct answers.**

1 Who was born in the Arctic Circle?
  a Marcia. b John.
2 Where did Marcia move when she was ten?
  a To Canada. b To the UK.
3 When did Marcia become a professional photographer?
  a When she was 16. b After she finished university.
4 Has John seen Marcia's photos of the aurora borealis?
  a Yes, he has. b No, he hasn't.
5 Why does Marcia take photos of animals?
  a She doesn't like taking photos of people. b She thinks that they might become extinct in the future.
6 Who says that the Arctic habitat may be in danger?
  a John. b Marcia.

2 18 **Listen and circle the correct words.**

1 Julie *is celebrating* / *may celebrate* her birthday on Friday.
2 Julie's sister *is going* / *might go* to the cinema with her.
3 There *are* / *may be* some films about the North and South poles at the Phoenix.
4 Leah *would* / *wouldn't* like to see the film about animals.
5 Leah thinks that Julie *won't* / *may* choose *Northern Lights and Home*.
6 Leah and Tom *will* / *may* meet again on Sunday.

Speaking

1 **Work with a friend. Imagine you are going on a trip to the Arctic. What might you see?**

I think we might see walruses.

I agree. But we won't see …

emperor penguin

walrus

southern elephant seal

polar bear

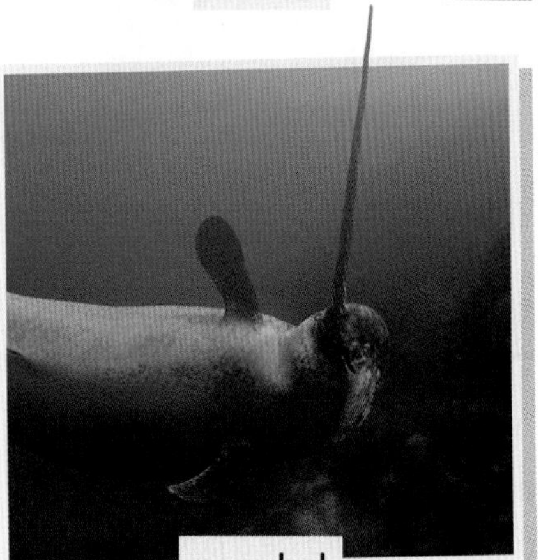
narwhal

Adélie penguin

2 **Think of three more animals that you might see in the Arctic. Share your ideas with your friend.**

We might see Arctic foxes!

That's right! And we may find …

3 **Think of the top three activities that you would like to do in the Arctic. Share your ideas with your friend.**

I'd like to see the aurora borealis. I'd also like to sleep in an igloo and take photos of seal pups. What about you?

I'd love to …

9 2nd conditional

Language focus

Use the **2nd conditional** to talk about imagined events or states.

They can either be unlikely *(**If I went** into space, I **would visit** the moon)* or impossible *(**If I were** an animal, I **would be** a lion).*

These sentences are formed in the following way:

If + **past simple** + **would** + **infinitive without to**.

It is possible to say *If I / he / she / it* ***were*** … or *If I / he / she / it* ***was*** …

1 Circle the correct verb form.

1. If I *meet* / *met* a famous person, I wouldn't take a photograph of them.
2. If I *could* / *can* go back in time, I'd visit Ancient Athens.
3. If I could fly, I'd *go* / *going* to the top of Mount Everest.
4. If I *had* / *have* time, I'd learn to play chess.
5. If we didn't have school tomorrow, I'd *went* / *go* snowboarding in the mountains.
6. If I were rich, I'd *gave* / *give* all my money away.

2 Order the sentences to make a story.

a If I got really tired, I'd sit in my basket. ____
b If I fell asleep, I'd dream about chasing cats. ____
c If I ran around in parks all day, I'd get tired. ____
d If I woke up from my dream, I'd realise I wasn't a dog. ____
e If I were a dog, I'd run around in parks. ____
f If I were an animal, I'd be a dog. 1
g If I sat in my basket, I'd fall asleep. ____

3 Complete the text with the verbs from the box in the correct form.

not be	read	can	not call	paint	not make	~~play~~	not need	remember	have

If, if, if ... Sometimes I think that 'if' is my favourite word. If I (1) **played** better, for example, I'd get into the school football team. If I were taller, people (2) ____ me 'shorty', and if I had a talent for painting, I (3) ____ my dreams. If I (4) ____ run fast, I would never miss the bus to school, and if I were good at Maths, I (5) ____ to ask Bonnie Mackintosh to help me. If I (6) ____ money, I would be able to buy that beautiful piano that's on display in the window of the music shop. If there was more time, I (7) ____ all the books I've got beside my bed, and if I had a really good memory, I (8) ____ everything I read instead of forgetting it all straightaway. But I suppose there is another way of looking at all of this ... If I (9) ____ sentences beginning with 'if' all the time, I (10) ____ me.

4 Complete the sentences with your own ideas.

1 If I could fly, ____.
2 If I could be anything, ____.
3 If I had a time machine, ____.
4 If I had all the money in the world, ____.
5 If I were a dinosaur, ____.

2nd conditional questions

Language focus

Use **2nd conditional questions** to ask someone what they would do in unlikely or impossible situations. These questions are formed in the following way:

Question word (**what**, **who**, **where**, etc.) + **would** + **infinitive without to** + **if** + **past simple**

What would you say if you met *the president of the United States of America?*

1 **Complete the questions with the verbs from the box in the correct form.**

be	~~can~~	own	visit	see	have

1 What would you do if you ___could___ do any job?
2 What would you do if you ____________ rich?
3 What would you do if you ____________ New York?
4 What would you do if you ____________ four extra hours every day?
5 What would you do if you ____________ a space rocket?
6 What would you do if you ____________ a tiger in the street?

2 **Match answers a–f with the questions from Activity 1.**

a I would give the money to people who need it. ____
b I would fly all the way to the moon. ____
c I'd make beautiful things out of wood and sell them for lots of money. __1__
d I'd climb a tree and then say, 'Hello.' ____
e I would sleep. ____
f I would take photographs of the skyscrapers. ____

3 **Complete the dialogue with the verbs from the box in the correct form.**

meet go ~~do~~ have ask be

Francois	Have you seen this website? There are lots and lots of questions – you know, what would you (1) ____do____ if … ?
Max	Ask me one.
Francois	What would you (2) ________ if you could be anything?
Max	Easy. Footballer. They make so much money. What about you?
Francois	I'd be a painter, I think. OK. Another question – if you (3) ________ Lionel Messi, what would you say to him?
Max	I'd ask him if he thinks he is better than Ronaldo. What about you?
Francois	I don't think I'd like to meet him. All right – ready for another one?
Max	Go on.
Francois	Where would you (4) ________ if you could live anywhere in the world?
Max	Hmm … that's an interesting one. I think I'd live in Vancouver.
Francois	OK, on we go. If you (5) ________ lots of money, what would you do with it?
Max	I think I'd invent a new kind of spaceship and travel to distant galaxies.
Francois	Last one – if you could (6) ________ me any question, what would you ask?
Max	When's lunch?

4 **Answer the questions.**

1 What would you do if you could have any job?

____

2 What ability would you like to have if you could have any ability?

____

3 Who would you meet if you could meet anyone?

____

4 Where would you go if you could go anywhere?

____

Reading: an online message board

1 **Read the comments on the online forum and answer the questions.**

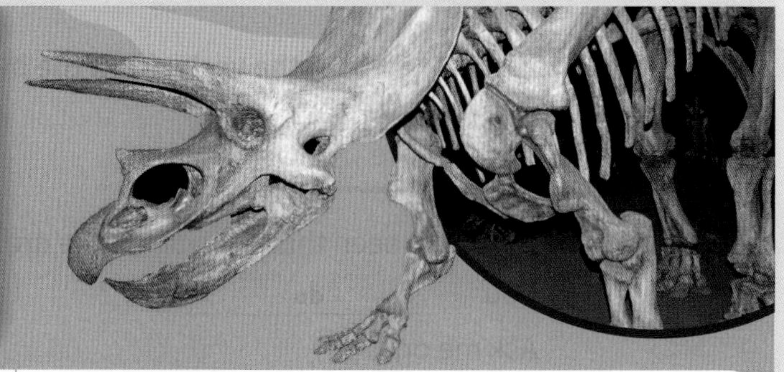

where dinosaur fans talk dinosaurs

Discussion question: If you went back to the time of the dinosaurs, what would you do?

From FredtheFossil Posted 4.12 p.m.
I'd get away as fast as my legs could carry me! I don't think our dinosaur friends would be interested in a chat!

From BrontySaurus Posted 4.13 p.m.
LOL! Great question. What would I do? I don't know! Take a photo from behind a big bush.

From MeRex Posted 4.18 p.m.
I'd jump into a swamp, throw stones at the dinosaurs and then go 'rahhhhhhhh' to see if any of the creatures got scared and ran away.

From JurassicMark Posted 4.30 p.m.
Hey, MeRex. I've got another question for you – if one of the dinosaurs shouted 'rahhhhhhh' at you, what would you do? LMK.

From TheTerribleLizard Posted 5.00 p.m.
Can't wait to discuss the question, but I've got to have dinner now. BRB.

From HerbieVore Posted 5.01 p.m.
IMO, IRL, we would all be really scared and wouldn't know what to do. Imagine – no Internet, no phones, no TV, and lots of huge dinosaurs running after us!

From PerryDactyl Posted 5.10 p.m.
Great question but can I ask a different one? Has anyone played Sunrise Horizon? It's a new dinosaur video game. LMK.

From Swampy Posted 6.33 p.m.
Hi, PerryDactyl. I have! It's brilliant! DM me and I'll send you a link to it.

1 Who says it would be very scary for everyone? HerbieVore
2 Who can't answer the question because they have to eat something? ______
3 Who can help someone with information about a new game? ______
4 Who would shout at the dinosaurs? ______
5 Who has another question? ______ and ______
6 Who would run away? ______

1 **Match Internet abbreviations 1–6 with phrases a–f.**

1 LOL	a be right back	____
2 LMK	b in my opinion	____
3 IMO	c laugh / laughing out loud	1
4 BRB	d direct message	____
5 DM	e in real life	____
6 IRL	f let me know	____

Help with Writing

Abbreviations are a common feature of communication on the Internet. It is a good idea to learn some in English that you can use if you chat to people in forums.

2 **Choose a question to discuss.**

- If you were a dinosaur, which one would you be?
- If you could have a special power, which one would you choose?
- If you could fly, where would you go?

Write comments from people in response to the question. Include the following:

- a name for each contributor
- a time they posted their contribution
- a reason for each answer.

Listening: travelling through time

1 19 **Listen and put Tim's story in order.**

- [ ] Tim chose to travel to the Jurassic Period.
- [ ] Tim and Cynthia saw a stegosaurus.
- [1] Last week, Tim's mum, Cynthia, invented a time machine.
- [ ] Tim pressed some red buttons and a blue switch.
- [ ] The time machine shook and everything went dark.
- [ ] Cynthia pressed the 'Go' key on the keypad.
- [ ] Tim and Cynthia stood on grassland and watched the sun rise.

2 20 **Listen to the conversation. Write *t* (true) or *f* (false).**

1 If Mila had lots of money, she'd buy a laptop and a new games console. [f]
2 Ethan doesn't know Tim's mum. [ ]
3 Ethan would like to be an Egyptian pharaoh. [ ]
4 If Mila had a time machine, she'd go into space with Neil Armstrong. [ ]
5 Ethan would like to hunt big woolly mammoths. [ ]
6 Ethan and Mila would like to travel to the future. [ ]

1 **Work with a friend. Read about Cynthia Wade's time machine. Then choose your questions and ask and answer.**

CYNTHIA WADE'S Time Machine

The world's first time machine is now open to the public!

If you could travel back in time, where would you go? Get on this amazing time machine and choose your favourite time period: Ancient Rome, Ancient Egypt, London before the Great Fire, the Jurassic Period … The choice is *yours!*

Come and live this fantastic experience. Visit us on Saturdays and Sundays, from 10 a.m. to 1 p.m. **Price:** £10 an hour.

Student A

- Has anyone invented a time machine before?
- When can you use the time machine?

Student B

- Which time periods does the advertisement suggest visiting?
- If you wanted to travel for two hours, how much would you have to pay?

2 **With your friend, talk about two time periods that you would like to visit.**

Where would you go if you had a time machine?

I'd go to the Stone Age and I'd go to the time of the Incas in South America. What about you?

3 **Do you think inventing a time machine is a good idea? Why? Why not? Say three reasons.**

I don't think inventing a time machine is a good idea. If a time machine was invented, it would be dangerous because …

Audioscripts

Welcome Unit page 10

01

Mum Have you packed your bag yet, George?

George Yes, I've already done that, Mum. I think I've got everything for my first day.

Mum Great. Do you remember the information that we read about the school?

George Yes, I think so. Miss Green is one of our teachers. She teaches Year Six four days a week.

Mum That's right. We're going to meet Miss Green this morning, before school starts. Now, what about Mr Martin?

George Mr Martin is the other Year Six teacher. He's the one who we've got on Fridays.

Mum Great. Can you tell me about the homework box?

George Yes. The homework box is where you put your homework on Monday mornings. You don't give your work to the teacher.

Mum OK! There's one more thing. After we meet Miss Green, we're going to meet a girl called Katy. Do you remember?

George Oh, yes! Katy is the classmate who is going to show me around the school.

Mum That's right. Oh! Can you make your bed now, George? Then we'll go.

George OK, Mum!

02

Katy Hi, George. I'm Katy. It's nice to meet you!

George Hello, Katy. Nice to meet you, too!

Katy Welcome to your new school. Everyone in our class is very friendly. Have you met Miss Green yet?

George Yes, I have. I met her when I arrived.

Katy Great! OK, let me show you around our school. Follow me!

George Wow! That is a big running track! I love running races.

Katy Me too! And look at that – that's the football pitch where we play matches every Tuesday.

George Fantastic! I'm really good at football. And I also like tennis!

Katy Hmm ... There aren't any tennis courts here. But the school has got a playground with lots of basket hoops in it. Do you like basketball?

George Yes, I do. I'm not very good at it, but I like playing it.

Katy OK, great. Hmm ... Ah! We've got a new gym – that's where we have some of our PE lessons.

George Yes, I've already seen the gym. Miss Green showed it to me this morning. It looks amazing!

Katy Brilliant! Now, let's go back inside. I'd like to take you to the place where you can find lots of interesting books: the library!

George Sounds good! But just one question – I'd like to come to school by bike some days. Is there a place where I can leave my bike?

Katy No, there aren't any bike racks at school. You'll have to cycle at the weekend.

George OK. That's fine.

Unit 1 page 18

03

Come with me to the days of adventure on the high seas! On one bright morning, Master Bob, the leader of a famous pirate gang, was lying in his hammock. 'Samuel,' he said to the youngest pirate in the gang, 'how long have we been pirates?' Samuel scratched his head with the hook where his right hand used to be. Then he said, 'We've been pirates for 13 years, Master Bob – 13 fabulous years!' The two men laughed. They loved to find treasure chests on sandy beaches, then relax in the sun under the palm trees. 'All I need to be happy now,' said Master Bob, 'is some new gold coins and the smell of salt in the wind. What a life we live, Samuel. What a—' At that moment, there was a loud noise. Master Bob sat up. 'All pirates on deck!' he shouted. But before Master Bob could get out of his hammock, he saw a woman climb onto the ship. Then she stepped forward. 'I'm Mary Ann of the North,' the woman said, 'and this boat is now mine!' Mary Ann moved her blue eye-patch down over the hole where her left eye used to be. She was scary! The easy life of Master Bob and his pirate gang was about to change ...

04

Helen When's your next show, Freddie?

Freddie Oh, very soon, Helen – at the weekend! It's a comedy about pirates. And it's called *Pirates*.

Helen That's funny! How long have you been practising for it?

Freddie I've been practising for three months. I'm going to be a pirate called Captain Stone. He's very brave and a little silly!

Helen That sounds great.

Freddie Yes. I love going to drama club. I started when I was a little boy.

Helen Really? How old were you?

Freddie I was five! I've acted in lots of plays since then.

Helen How many?

Freddie Hmm ... Six. Six plays. One play every year.

Helen That sounds fun. I don't go to the theatre very often. I can't remember the last time I went!

Freddie Why don't you come to see *Pirates*?

Helen Of course! I'd love to! I've got a party on Saturday, but I can go to the Sunday show. I'll ask my brother to come with me.

Freddie Great, Helen! See you there!

Helen See you on Sunday, Captain Stone!

Unit 2 page 26

05

Hello! I'm Professor Lucy Mayweather, and I'm going to talk about the future of travel. So, in the future, do you think that people will travel more than they do today? Well, I think that we will travel less! Why? Because we will be more interested in saving the planet. Some modern types of transport, like cars and planes, have polluted the environment for years. So, I think that we won't use these types of transport in the future, and we won't need them to move around. People won't travel long distances – so they will use cable cars, monorails or electric bikes for short trips. And thanks to the Internet, we will communicate easily with friends and family in other cities or countries. We won't need to fly or drive to visit them. Now, have you got any questions at this point? What do you think? Let me hear your ideas.

06

Ivy Have you watched the video of Professor Mayweather yet, Leo?

Leo The presentation about the future of travel? Yes, I have, Ivy.

Ivy What did you think of it?

Leo Hmm ... Some of the professor's ideas were interesting, but I don't agree with all of them.

Ivy I see what you mean. I'd like to travel to other countries in the future! And I need to take a plane to see my cousins in Australia. I can't go by monorail!

Leo Hahaha! I agree. I think that we will need planes to travel around the world. Perhaps there will be planes that don't pollute the environment so much.

Ivy That's right! I read about some planes that use energy from the sun. They're called solar-powered planes.

Leo Solar-powered planes? That sounds cool! I'd like to fly in one of those.

Ivy Me too. And I like the idea that we will get on cable cars to move around. That will be fun!

Leo Yes! And I will also use my birthday present to go to school every day.

Ivy Your birthday present? What is it? Oh, let me guess: a microlight!

Leo Haha. Very funny! No, it isn't. It's a floating skateboard!

Ivy That's really cool!

Unit 3 page 34

07

Milly Hey, Connor. I'm reading a great book. Look – it's called *The History of Ancient Egypt*.

Connor It looks interesting!

Milly It is! I've got only five more pages to read.

Connor Oh! So I can test you then!

Milly Test me?

Connor Yes! We can see what you remember.

Milly OK. We've only got a little time, though.

Connor Let's start. Great. There are lots of facts on this page. Right. Where were the pharaohs buried?

Milly I know that one! They were buried in pyramids. Most pyramids were tombs for important people in Ancient Egypt.

Connor Correct. OK. Next question. Where in Egypt were the most famous pyramids built?

Milly They were built in Giza, near Cairo.

Connor Yes! And the last question – who were the pyramids built by?

Milly They were built by slaves. They had to move lots of blocks of rock in the hot sun … Now I've got a question for you, Connor. But you can't look in the book.

Connor I'm ready!

Milly What do you call Ancient Egyptian writing?

Connor Hmm … I know that people used symbols, but I can't remember … What were they called?

Milly Hieroglyphs!

Connor That's right!

08

Every day, everything was done for the pharaoh. His hands and feet were washed, his meals were prepared and he was dressed in a headdress and jewellery. Then the pharaoh was taken around in his chariot. His life was easy, but it was a little boring. 'I've got a lot of time,' the pharaoh said, 'but I haven't got anything interesting to do.' One day, the pharaoh asked his favourite slave to come to him. 'I want to know what it is like to be a slave,' he said. 'Please change places with me.' And so the slave became the pharaoh and the pharaoh became a slave. Now, nothing was done for the pharaoh. He didn't have time to wash and he ate very little. He wore a few simple clothes and spent his day moving heavy rocks for the new pyramid. His life was hard. 'I've got very little time,' he said, 'and a lot of work to do.' The pharaoh didn't want to be a slave any more. He said, 'I'm the pharaoh. Take me back to the palace,' but people laughed at him. So he had to keep carrying heavy rocks under the sun to build a pyramid for the man who used to be his slave.

Unit 4 page 42

09

Alex Are you enjoying the Olympic week at school, Holly?

Holly Yes, of course! I loved the gymnastics lesson.

Alex My favourite has been the archery event. It was fun! Hey, we could try doing an Olympic sport together.

Holly Good idea! Which one?

Alex Let's see … We could try weightlifting – it's on Wednesday.

Holly Hmm … I'm not sure. I don't like lifting weights … But we could try boxing. It's on Wednesday, too.

Alex Hmm … My brother wants to do boxing, but I don't like fighting.

Holly OK. What about fencing? We would fight, but with swords! It could be fun!

Alex OK! I don't mind fighting with swords. And what about going to the hurdles competition? It's on Thursday. We could do that and then do some rowing in the afternoon.

Holly Good idea. And after rowing we could try some wrestling.

Alex Wrestling? No way! I don't like fighting. I told you, Holly …

Holly Hahaha! I know, Alex. I was joking!

10

Coach OK, Sophie. Have you planned your training schedule for next week?

Sophie Yes, I have, Coach.

Coach Well done! You're working hard! Let's talk about the schedule, then. What are you doing on Monday?

Sophie I'm swimming at five o'clock, after school.

Coach Great. What about Tuesday?

Sophie On Tuesday I'm swimming too. But I'm doing it in the morning, before school.

Coach What time?

Sophie At half past seven.

Coach That's an early start! Make sure you go to bed early on Monday.

Sophie OK, Coach. Then on Wednesday I'm doing gymnastics at quarter to six in the afternoon.

Coach Gymnastics on Wednesday sounds brilliant. So we've only got Thursday left. What are you doing on Thursday?

Sophie On Thursday I'm practising the long jump. The long jump is the most difficult sport for me. But I'm going with my sister, so it will be fun.

Coach That's great. What time are you doing that?

Sophie At quarter past four in the afternoon.

Coach Fantastic. That looks like a good plan for the week. Then you have Friday and the weekend to relax and have fun!

Sophie Sure, Coach!

Unit 5 page 50

11

Miss Collins Good morning, everyone. Today, we're going to talk about cities around the world. First, let's find out about you and the cities that you know. Who has ever been to a city in North or South America? OK, Jane?

Jane I've been to New York, Miss Collins. I went there last summer, with my parents.

Miss Collins Great! So Jane has been to New York. What about a city in Europe? Have you ever been to any? Yes, Jacob?

Jacob I've been to Rome, in Italy.

Miss Collins Good! Did you like it?

Jacob Yes, I did! I like finding out all about the Ancient Romans. Rome was the perfect place for me!

Miss Collins I can imagine that. You know I love Ancient Egypt, so I've been to Cairo three times. Yes, Carmen?

Carmen Like me, Miss Collins! I've never been to Cairo, but I've been to London three times.

Miss Collins Of course, Carmen. You've got family there.

Carmen Yes. My grandparents live in London. I stayed with them last December.

Miss Collins That's right, I remember. How long were you there?

Carmen I was there for two weeks. I loved it! We went to Tower Bridge, the London Eye and Madame Tussauds, but my favourite place was the Tower of London. It was very interesting!

Miss Collins It is really interesting, I agree! OK, now let's talk about different cities …

12

Emma Hi, Max. What are you looking at?

Max Oh, just some photos of London. I went there last summer.

Emma Cool! How long were you there?

Max I was there for a week.

Emma Did you go with your dad?

Max Yes, I did. We stayed with my aunt. She lives there now.

Emma Oh! So, did you have a good time?

Max Yes! I really liked being with my aunt. She took us to lots of great places and we did lots of fun things.

Emma That sounds nice! So which thing was your favourite?

Max Hmm … I loved the parks in London. They're really big and beautiful. But the best thing was a film that we saw.

Emma A film?

Max Yes. It was about the Great Fire of London. Have you ever heard of it?

Emma Of course! We were talking about that in school. Do you remember?

Max That's right! Well, the film was very interesting. And it was at a really cool cinema. There were screens on all four walls of this big room! And on each screen, you could see the London streets with old shops. Imagine a chemist's, a tailor's, a carpenter's … from 1666! Then after the film, my aunt took me to a nice baker's and we had delicious cake.

Emma Wow! It all sounds great.

Max Yes. Oh! And there were smells in the cinema room, too!

Emma Smells? What do you mean?

Max Yes, from the London streets. Imagine what London smelt like in the 17th century!

Emma What did it smell like?

Max Terrible!

Unit 6 page 58

13

Hi! I'm Molly, and I'd like to tell you about Cynthia Wade. Cynthia is my aunt's friend. She is an amazing inventor, but she's a little crazy. She has invented a flying car, walking shoes and an umbrella that never breaks in the wind! Well, last weekend, I went to Cynthia's laboratory. I'd like to be a famous inventor one day and I wanted to watch her work. The room was a mess! There were too many paint pots on the floor. And on a long workbench, there were screwdrivers and spanners. In the middle of the room, there was a big table with some hammers and nails on it. One of Cynthia's assistants was holding a drill and another one was using a paintbrush. Then Cynthia said, 'There are too many things in this room, and there isn't enough space. Please take the paint pots out. Quickly!' The assistants started carrying the paint pots out of the laboratory. Then Cynthia pressed a switch on the wall and the room became really dark. 'That's better,' she said, and she sat down on the floor. Then she said, 'When I'm ready, I'll know what to invent.' Suddenly, Cynthia stood up, turned on the lights and said, 'I've got it! I'll invent a machine that keeps toast warm! Assistants, come back in here, please!'

14

Cynthia Molly, are you tired? You've been here for six hours!

Molly I'm OK, Cynthia. I've enjoyed watching you at work.

Cynthia That's good to know. So, have you got any questions? What would you like to know?

Molly Sure! OK. Can you tell me what that big grey machine is?

Cynthia That's a super-computer. It's one of the most powerful machines in the world.

Molly Wow! Can you tell me what the red switch does?

Cynthia Of course. When I press the switch, I can talk to my assistants in the other room.

Molly I see. What about that yellow lever? Can you tell me what it's for?

Cynthia Yes, of course. When I push up the lever, my workbench moves from there to there. Look.

Molly Great! Did you invent that?

Cynthia Of course I did!

Molly I knew it! So how did you decide to become an inventor?

Cynthia That's an interesting question. My mother was an inventor. I enjoyed creating things with her. She taught me how to use drills, spanners, screwdrivers and saws. It was fun!

Molly I'm sure it was! One day I'd like to be an inventor. I like drawing pictures of machines and objects.

Cynthia Well, imagination and creativity are the main ingredients of good inventions. Would you like to show me your pictures?

Molly Of course! I'll bring them next time.

Cynthia Brilliant!

Unit 7 page 66

15

James Going to museums is fun, Dad. But I think this is the best museum in the world!

Dad I said that it was good, James!

James You were right!

Dad Look, James! This is a lunar module. Neil Armstrong and Edwin Aldrin travelled in one in 1969. Can you believe it?

James I know, Dad! It's very, very small! I think leaving the moon in that was uncomfortable!

Dad Hmm … Look at this. I think it's a countdown clock. Let's see … Yes, it says here that it is a countdown clock.

James Do you mean the clock that astronauts use when they say 'ten, nine, eight, seven …'?

Dad Yes, that's right.

James Wow! Hey, look! Over there – next to the photos of craters on the moon. It's a spacesuit! How cool!

Dad It looks fantastic. Let's go and see it.

James Seeing it is great, but can you imagine wearing it?

Dad That would be amazing! Would you like to be an astronaut, James?

James Hmm … No, Dad. I love learning all about space, but I think working as an astronaut is very difficult.

Dad I agree. Travelling to the moon is not an easy job! Right, shall we have a break now? Walking around museums is tiring. Let's have some lunch in the museum café. We could try their space sandwiches!

James Mmm … Great idea, Dad!

16

Helen You know, Henry, my brother had a strange dream last night. He said that in his dream, he saw an alien!

Henry Really, Helen? Tell me more!

Helen Well, my brother said that he was in the park. He said that he was with our dog.

Henry So what happened?

Helen Well, he said that suddenly, a space capsule landed next to the lake.

Henry And what happened after that? Did a little green creature come out of the capsule?

Helen Haha! Very funny. Well, he said that a tall yellow alien stepped out of the capsule. It was a girl alien, and she was very nice. She had some blue spots on her hands and feet.

Henry Amazing! So what did your brother do?

Helen He said that he spoke to the alien, in English! He said hello and the alien understood. Then the alien touched the dog. She was friendly.

Henry OK. So what happened next? Did they all go for a swim in the lake?

Helen Don't be silly. We don't know what happened next because … that's when my brother woke up.

Henry Oh, well. I think your brother should write down this dream – and he could create an ending for it.

Helen Guess what? He had the same idea! So next time, I'll tell you how the story ends!

Unit 8 page 74

17

John Welcome to *Zoom*, Radio Nine's photography show. I'm John White and photographer Marcia Lee is with me today. Her pictures of the Arctic Circle are very famous around the world. Hello, Marcia.

Marcia Hi, John. Thanks for inviting me on the show.

John Thank you for coming! Now, you are from the Arctic Circle, aren't you?

Marcia Yes, I am. I was born in Cambridge Bay in the far north of Canada. I spent the first ten years of my life there. Then I moved to the UK.

John Interesting. When did you become a photographer?

Marcia I started taking photos when I was 16. Then I studied photography at university and became a professional photographer after that.

John You were young! And when did you start taking photos of the Arctic Circle?

Marcia Well, after university, I moved to Iceland. From Iceland, I began travelling around the Arctic Circle and taking photos. I haven't stopped since then!

John Sounds exciting! Tell us, what do you like about the North Pole?

Marcia The wonderful animals, of course. And the special light – the aurora borealis is amazing, isn't it?

John Yes, it is. Your photos show that. And you've taken some fantastic pictures of polar bears and seals.

Marcia Thanks. I used to take photos of people, too. But these days I only take photos of animals. I want people to see them – they might disappear in the future.

John You're right. The ice in the North Pole is melting quickly. If we don't act now, the Arctic habitat may be in serious trouble.

18

Tom What are you doing on Friday, Leah?

Leah It's Julie's birthday. We're going to the cinema!

Tom That sounds fun! Who's going?

Leah Julie, Anna and me. Oh, and Julie's mum is coming too. Julie's sister doesn't know yet – she's got another birthday party on that day!

Tom Oh dear! You are all very busy! So, what are you going to see?

Leah Well, Julie hasn't decided yet. The Phoenix is showing different films about the North and South poles.

Tom That sounds interesting.

Leah One is a film about animals. I really want to see that one! There are polar bears and seals, with their cubs and pups. There are penguins and Arctic foxes, too.

Tom That sounds nice. You really love animals!

Leah I do! Then there's a comedy called *Northern Lights and Home*. It's about an Inuit family who live in Greenland.

Tom Hmm … I think I'd like to see that one.

Leah Well, Julie also really likes comedies, doesn't she? So I think we may see *Northern Lights and Home* in the end.

Tom You may be right! But you know what? I think you'll have a great time. Tell me about it on Sunday!

Leah I will! See you on Sunday, Tom!

Unit 9 page 82

19

What would you do if you met a dinosaur? Well, I met a dinosaur last week. How? My mum is an inventor. Her name is Cynthia Wade. Last week, Mum invented … a time machine! It didn't look like a very special machine, but it worked! Mum said, 'Tim, get on the time machine with me. Where would you like to go?' And so we went to the Jurassic Period, my favourite! I pressed two small red buttons, then pressed a big blue switch and my mum wrote, '160 million years ago' on the keypad. After that, she pressed the 'Go' key. We shook for about five seconds and everything went dark! Suddenly, we were standing on grassland and watching the sun rise on the horizon. It was really hot! There were swamps around us. And then we saw it, walking straight towards us through the trees: a stegosaurus! At first, I thought we could hide behind a log or a bush, or jump into the stream behind us, but then I said, 'Mum! Please! Press the "Home" button now!'

20

Mila Ethan, what would your life be like if …

Ethan If what, Mila?

Mila I don't know … if you lived in another time. Or if you had lots of money. Or if you saw a T-rex. You know, if things were different.

Ethan Well! If I had lots of money, I'd buy a laptop and a new games console and …

Mila OK, OK. Wait. Do you know Tim's mum?

Ethan Yes – Cynthia. She's an inventor, isn't she?

Mila Yes, she is. Well, she's invented a time machine. Tim said that they went back to the Jurassic Period!

Ethan Really? What did they see?

Mila They saw a stegosaurus! Now, listen. If you got on that time machine, where would you go?

Ethan Well, let me think … I'd go to Ancient Egypt. I'd become an Egyptian pharaoh. What about you? What would you do?

Mila I think I'd travel to the moon with Neil Armstrong.

Ethan Wow! That's a great choice.

Mila I know! And after that, I'd go to the Stone Age.

Ethan Amazing! You'd be a hunter-gatherer.

Mila That's right. I'd hunt big woolly mammoths. What about you? Where would you travel after Ancient Egypt?

Ethan After Ancient Egypt … I wouldn't go back in time again. I'd go forward – to the future!

Mila Cool! I'd love to travel to the future, too. Let's go together!

Acknowledgements

The authors and publishers acknowledge the following sources of copyright material and are grateful for the permissions granted. While every effort has been made, it has not always been possible to identify the sources of all the material used, or to trace all copyright holders. If any omissions are brought to our notice, we will be happy to include the appropriate acknowledgements on reprinting and in the next update to the digital edition, as applicable.

Key: ST = Starter; U = Unit

Photography

The following images are sourced from Getty Images.

ST: BanksPhotos/iStock/Getty Images Plus; db2stock; clubfoto/iStock/Getty Images Plus; SDI Productions/E+; wakila/E+; Picsfive/iStock/Getty Images Plus; nycshooter/iStock/Getty Images Plus; EJ_Rodriquez/iStock/Getty Images Plus; izusek/iStock/Getty Images Plus; **U1:** Hill Street Studios/DigitalVision; **U2:** ktsimage/iStock/Getty Images Plus; Henglein and Steets/Cultura; narvikk/E+; KevinHyde/iStock/Getty Images Plus; **U3:** exipreess/iStock/Getty Images Plus; WitR/iStock/Getty Images Plus; majaiva/iStock/Getty Images Plus; LUke1138/iStock/Getty Images Plus; **U4:** exipreess/iStock/Getty Images Plus; Granger Wootz; askPdesigns/iStock/Getty Images Plus; FatCamera/E+; suemack/iStock/Getty Images Plus; **U5:** gojak/iStock/Getty Images Plus; Tony Evans/Timelapse Library Ltd/Hulton Archive; Vladislav Zolotov/iStock/Getty Images Plus; Dorling Kindersley; PeopleImages/iStock/Getty Images Plus; Jetta Productions Inc/DigitalVision; Johner Images; RossHelen/iStock/Getty Images Plus; sturti/E+; LightFieldStudios/iStock/Getty Images Plus; **U6:** Andy Nowack/iStock/Getty Images Plus; Peter Stark; eleonora galli/Moment; Sharad Bapat/500px; JurgaR/E+; AndreyPopov/iStock/Getty Images Plus; Witthaya Prasongsin/Moment; Gregor Schuster/Photographer's Choice RF; Rob Lewine; **U7:** Cavan Images; World Perspectives/The Image Bank/Getty Images Plus; Nerthuz/iStock/Getty Images Plus; mchlhills/iStock/Getty Images Plus; 3DSculptor/iStock/Getty Images Plus; **U8:** Danita Delimont/Gallo Images/Getty Images Plus; Scott Frew/500px; Wayne R Bilenduke/The Image Bank/Getty Images Plus; Martin Ruegner/Stone; zanskar/iStock/Getty Images Plus; Holger Leue/The Image Bank; Yvette Cardozo/Stockbyte; dottedhippo/iStock/Getty Images Plus; Dr John A Horsfall/iStock/Getty Images Plus; **U9:** Warpaintcobra/iStock/Getty Images Plus; mikkelwilliam/iStock/Getty Images Plus.

The following image is sourced from another library.

ST: Iain Sarjeant/Alamy Stock Photo.

Illustrations

Sam Church; Mark Duffin; Graham Kennedy; Daniel Limon (Beehive Illustration); Alan Rowe (Beehive Illustration); Simon Rumble (Beehive Illustration); Dave Smith (Beehive Illustration).

Audio

All the audio clips are sourced from Getty Images.

Anton Orlov/Sound Effects; Benoit Daoust/Sound Effects; Cedric Hommel/Sound Effects; Christopher Jung David Hatton/Sound Effects; Derridon/Sound Effects; Francis Cerioni/Sound Effects; Hans Solgaard/Sound Effects; Ian Hubball/Sound Effects; Jonny Slatter/Sound Effects; José Tomé/Sound Effects; Lazar Zivanac/Sound Effects; LDj_Audio/Sound Effects; Reinhard Wedemeyer/Sound Effects; Robert Gacek/Sound Effects; Shawn Pigott/Sound Effects; Slobodan Levakov/Sound Effects; Sound Effects; Stefan Winkler/Sound Effects; Vage Petrosyan/Sound Effects; Zofia Pawlaczek/Sound Effects.

Audio production by Hart McLeod.

Typeset

EMC Design limited.

Cover design by We Are Bold.